Better Campin

Alan Ryalls has edited *Camping and Caravanning*, the magazine of the Camping Club of Great Britain, for many years and has written books and articles about camping and travel.

Roger Marchant works for the Association of Cycle and Lightweight Campers, a section of the Camping Club of Great Britain, and writes regularly in its journal.

Also available in Piccolo

BETTER NETBALL FOR GIRLS – Joyce Wheeler
BETTER RIDING – Lt.-Colonel 'Bill' Froud

Better camping

Alan Ryalls and Roger Marchant

With 125 photographs and line drawings

A PICCOLO BOOK

PAN BOOKS LTD
LONDON AND SYDNEY

First published 1973 by Kaye & Ward Ltd
This edition published 1975 by Pan Books Ltd
Cavaye Place, London SW10 9PG
ISBN 0 330 24356 X

Printed in Great Britain by
Butler & Tanner Ltd, Frome and London

Contents

Introduction 7
Basic requirements 9
  Pitching and packing 10
  Comfortable sleeping 22
  Cooking and lighting 28
  Hygiene 37
  Clothing 40
Back-packing 43
  A rucksack to suit 43
  A choice of footwear 48
  Weight watching 50
Cycle camping 55
Canoe camping 60
Mountain camping 67
Gadgets and comfort 76
When you're experienced 85
  Proficiency tests 85
  Winter camping 87
  International camping 90
Code for good camping 92
Equipment check list 93

Better Camping is dedicated to the members of the Association of Cycle and Lightweight Campers, founder body of the Camping Club of Great Britain and Ireland in 1901, to the members of the Canoe Camping Club and particularly to the many members of the Camping Club Youth who all co-operated so willingly in the production of the book. The members of these specialized sections of the Camping Club have played a major part in developing better camping.

Alan Ryalls
Roger Marchant

Acknowledgements

The pictures on pages 61, 74, 75, and 88 were kindly provided by Mr. E. Emrys Jones of Old Colwyn, and on pages 89 and 91 by Mrs. Kay Pitfield of the Camping Club Youth.

Most of the camping equipment used in the pictures was provided by Black and Edgington Ltd., Ruxley Corner, Sidcup, Kent. Tents were also provided by Pindisports, Vango, Ultimate and Easden Manufacturing Co.

The authors are grateful to these people for their help and co-operation in the preparation of this book.

Introduction

You've tried camping, you liked it and you'd like to do some more camping and do it better!

Well, that is what this book is all about. Read it, look carefully at the many pictures and diagrams, try out the suggestions and ideas and you'll find you get a lot more comfort and a lot more pleasure out of your camping in future.

We have both camped for many years, back-packing, cycling, canoeing, and we've learned to do it enjoyably and comfortably in all sorts of conditions.

When you have read this book, and started to put its ideas into practice, we hope you will enjoy your camping as much as we do.

Alan Ryalls
Roger Marchant

Basic requirements

In order to camp successfully and enjoyably you must have a good waterproof tent that is light enough to be easily portable but big enough to accommodate you (and maybe your friends) in reasonable comfort.

You must also have a reasonably strong and completely waterproof groundsheet, a warm but light and compact sleeping bag and, of course, a cooking stove, and pots and pans.

With these basics, you are able to camp satisfactorily and you will add your own choice of extras and accessories according to the type of camping you intend to do.

There is a wide choice of lightweight tents suitable for one, two or three campers. Most of them have a flysheet and there is no doubt that this adds tremendously to the comfort of your camping. A flysheet is a second roof suspended a few inches above the roof of your tent and extending well beyond the eaves, the rear end and the front. It gives great protection against driving rain, keeps your tent warmer in cold weather and cooler in hot weather and enables you to move about inside it more freely, and to touch the roof canvas sometimes without affecting its waterproofness. There is sheltered storage space under the edges of most flysheets as well.

The next point to consider is your groundsheet. Most lightweight tents have a sewn-in groundsheet and this is preferable because it ensures a completely waterproof link between tent and groundsheet. It also enables you to pitch the tent much more easily.

Your tent will be made of a lightweight cotton or nylon fabric, waterproofed and rotproofed or coated with silicones or polyurethane. The latter produces an absolutely waterproof material which cannot breathe, and a tent made entirely of this is subject to a great deal of condensation on the inside and so is not to be recommended. On the other hand, a polyurethane coated flysheet is fine because the condensation problem does not arise. An ideal combination is a tent with a siliconed roof, polyurethane coated walls and ends and an adequate ventilation system, used in conjunction with a polyurethane coated flysheet.

Finally, you should consider the type of poles for your tent. Most of the tents you will think of buying are supplied with light alloy poles which come in sections that slot into each other. Ideally, these poles should nest one inside the other for carrying. An A-pole is an optional extra with many lightweight tents. An A-pole straddles the tent which is suspended from it. This means that, in a single-pole tent, the whole of the floor space is usable and uncluttered. In a ridge tent, especially a sloping ridge tent, an A-pole at the front adds stability and leaves the entrance unimpeded. The disadvantage of an A-pole is that it can add 1½–2 pounds to the weight and £2·50–3·50 to the price. Unless weight is a vital factor an A-pole is to be recommended. So is a lightweight ridge pole which adds greatly to the set and stability of a ridge tent.

PITCHING AND PACKING

When you buy a new tent do not go straight off on a long camping holiday with it. Read the pitching instructions that should come with it and then pitch it in the garden or some other open space. This will teach you how to handle it. It is also a good idea to leave it pitched for a few days so that the canvas can weather and stretch a little. New tents may leak a bit until they have been out in the open for a few days.

If you decide to buy a tent with a sewn-in groundsheet, you will immediately see one advantage when you start to pitch it. You simply open up the groundsheet and spread it out, then peg down all the pegging points and the tent is anchored, ready for the insertion of

This series of pictures shows the stages in pitching a tent. The tent used is a Blacks Good Companions Standard tent with a flysheet and an A-pole. Weight 14 lb 8 oz; length 5 ft; width 7 ft; height 5 ft.

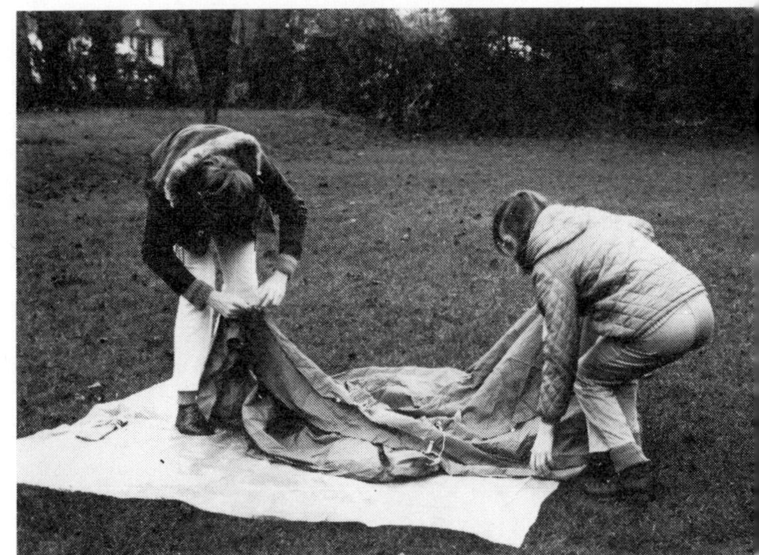

The tent is taken out of its carrying bag and opened up on a sheet of polythene. It is pegged down at the bottom, all round, and the corner guy-lines are loosely pegged out. A suspender is threaded through the hole in the peak of the tent and attached to the hook on the A-pole.

The A-pole is then erected, suspending the tent. Note that the entrance door is being zipped closed. This is essential for the correct pitching of a tent. The tent guylines are tightened and then the flysheet is spread over the tent and A-poles, without catching on the spike at the peak of the A-pole. The flysheet has a strengthened section at the peak, with a hole through which the spike is inserted.

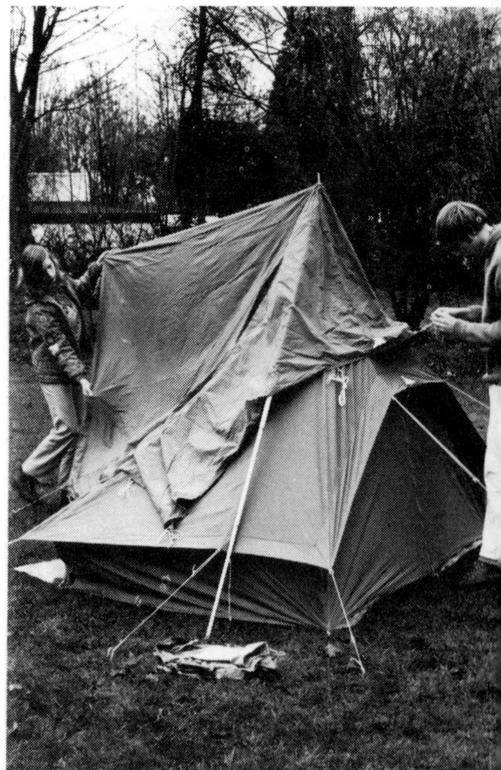

Now the flysheet is guyed out so that it takes on the shape of the tent but overhangs it all round. The guylines of the flysheet are tensioned and one or two pegs may have to be moved a little to ensure that the flysheet 'sits' properly.

The guylines of the porch are adjusted so that it 'sits' squarely over the doorway of the tent. When the flysheet and tent are fully pitched, the pegs are pushed firmly into the ground. Just one guyline remains to be pegged out in the final picture.

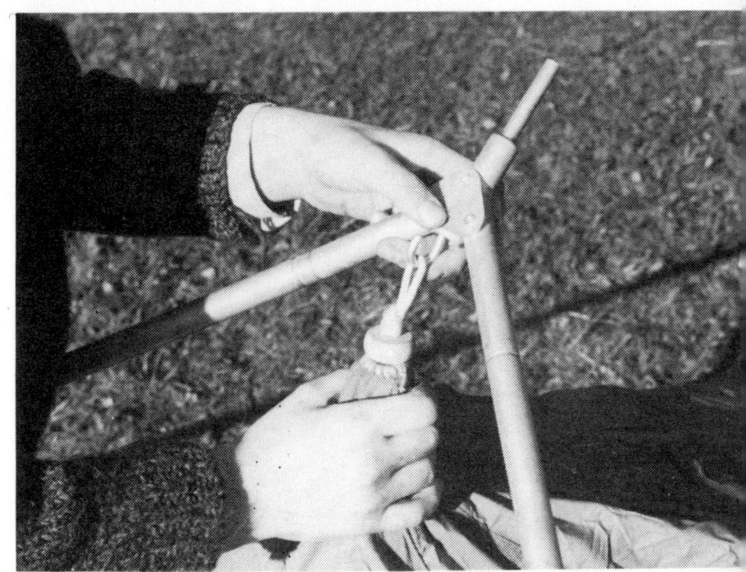

A 'close-up' of an A-pole showing the spike on which the fly-sheet 'sits' and the hook from which the tent is suspended.

When using a single pole, the pitching sequence is exactly the same except that the pole is inserted from the inside taking care that the pole spike does not snag the fabric.

The drawback with an internal upright pole is the loss of useful space taken up by it.

the pole(s). A single-pole tent with a sewn-in groundsheet will usually stand on its own as soon as you insert the pole and it is then an easy business to go round pegging out and adjusting the guylines so that the tent sits properly. You must extend the pole by adding a small extension piece that slots on the pole pip outside the tent, and then you are ready to put on the flysheet. Make sure that it is properly anchored over the extension pip before you start pegging out the guy-lines. The pictures show you how an A-pole is used. If you use a ridge pole on your ridge tent, it is slotted over the pips of the extenders (they are usually called 'separators') on your upright poles, and the flysheet is then slung over the ridge, anchored over the separator pips and pegged out.

How do you decide on the best spot to pitch your tent? Look at the ground and look at the weather. If the ground is uneven or sloping, choose the highest spot so that, if it rains, the water will run away from you. If the ground is yellowy-green and mossy it probably means it gets boggy in wet conditions, so look elsewhere. A slight depression can turn into a pool of water in wet weather and a tiny valley on a slope can become a watercourse.

Polythene sheeting is very useful to campers. A piece of thin polythene the size of your tent floor should always be carried. It protects the underside of your groundsheet from wear and mud and it gives you a clean surface on which to unpack and pack your tent.

Polythene sheeting is also useful for wrapping up your rucksack which sits outside smaller tents and could otherwise get wet.

The biggest enemy of lightweight campers is the wind, so always try to shelter from it. A hedge or a wall between you and the wind will make a lot of difference. So will a belt of trees—but don't camp under them, at any rate in Britain, because trees go on dripping long after rain has stopped and the drips from some trees can damage the fabric of your tent. So can falling branches and bird droppings. Anyway, you want to be out in the sun when it shines.

If the ground is sandy, it will absorb a lot of rain without becoming waterlogged. If it is heavy clay soil, the water may stay on the surface and in really bad conditions you might have to dig a shallow trench round your tent to lead the water away.

Most lightweight tents come with light steel or alloy pegs, some of them skewered to give a better grip. You can usually press them into the ground with your foot or knock them in with a stone. It is a good idea to carry a few V-section pegs because these hold well and may save your tent from blowing down in bad weather. When things are rough, don't hesitate to use spare guylines, doubling up your main guylines and the pegs holding them. Skewer pegs with a ring head can be made more secure by pushing another peg through the ring head at right angles to the peg holding the guy. If there is a firm anchorage, such as a tree or bush, nearby, you can always tie an extra guyline to it as an added precaution.

The Marechal Pedestra is a small ridge tent which has a sewn-in groundsheet that comes several inches up the walls to form a waterproof tray. The flysheet comes down almost to the ground. The door is closed by a single curved zip. The Pedestra is fine for two campers. Weight approximately 11½ lb.

The Blacks Oregon 107. This is a lightweight tent with a sloping ridge. When the rear (which is lower) is pitched into the wind, it helps to streamline the tent. It is made of nylon, with polyurethane coating on the doors and walls of the inner tent and on the whole of the flysheet. The roof of the inner tent is silicone proofed. An optional ridge pole improves its set and weighs 1 lb. An optional front A-pole in place of the single upright gives an unimpeded entrance and weighs $1\frac{1}{2}$ lb. Weight 6 lb 11 oz; length 7 ft; width, front 4 ft 6 in, rear 2 ft 3 in; height, front, 4 ft, rear 2 ft.

The flysheet of the Oregon has a deep porch that shelters the tent entrance in bad weather. You can cook under it in the rain.

This is the doorway of Blacks Good Companions tent showing an extra wedge-shaped piece of canvas at the bottom of the door. This allows the door to be pegged out so that it shelters the entrance and you can cook in its shelter in bad weather.

Packing up camp in the wet is not a particularly pleasant occupation but with a flysheet, especially one over a ridge pole or an A-pole, you can usually pack everything inside the tent, then drop the tent under the flysheet and pack it, leaving just the wet flysheet and pole. These can be bundled in the polythene sheet you placed under your groundsheet and the whole bundle can then be strapped on the outside of your rucksack, without causing any inconvenience. As an added precaution, and to save your rucksack from getting dirty, you could slip the whole bundle into a large polythene bag first.

If you are going straight home, don't forget to undo your wet tent and hang it out to dry as soon as you get there. But if you are going on camping, it will dry out the next time you pitch it.

It is always a good idea to air your tent after use. If it remains packed and wet for any length of time, the material may very well go mildewed and start to rot and then there is nothing you can do to reverse the process.

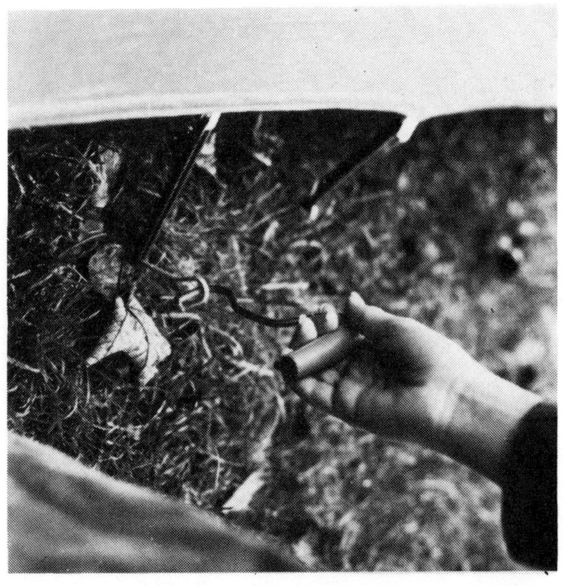

Sometimes pegs are difficult to extract from the ground. This is a small peg extractor with a hook to go under the peg hook, and a handle to pull.

If you don't have a peg extractor, use another peg. Insert it under the peg hook and you can then pull out the peg using both hands. Never use the guys to pull out pegs.

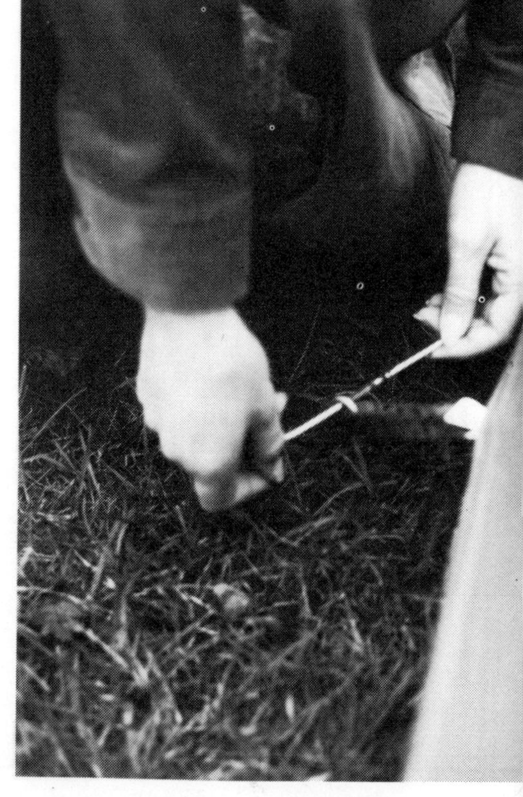

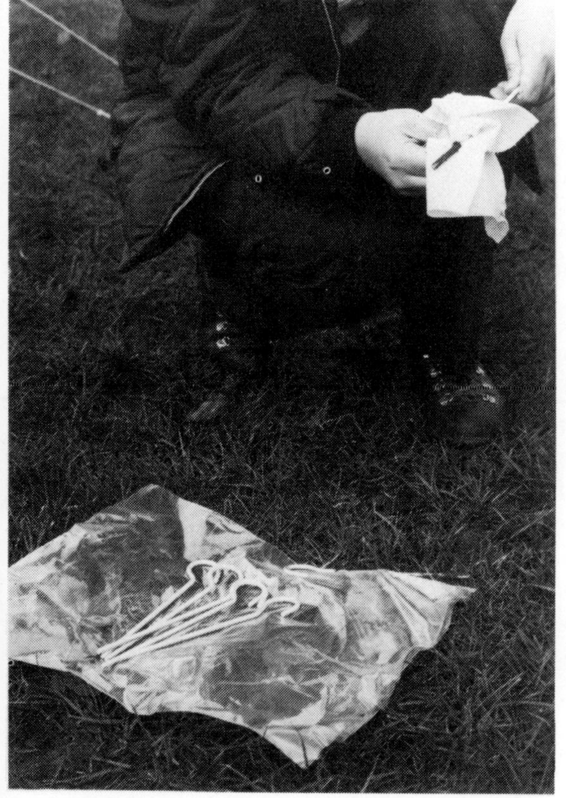

The camper is cleaning and counting the pegs in this picture. A tissue is used to clean off the mud that might otherwise dirty your tent when you pack up. The pegs are counted to ensure that all have been extracted. Thus, you will have sufficient pegs for your next camp—and you won't have left a peg in the ground for someone to trip over or to damage the feet of animals.

This section on pitching and packing may sound as though most camping is bad weather camping. In fact, quite the reverse is true, even in this country, and the odds are that you will rarely need to take any of the steps mentioned here—but it is as well to know how to.

COMFORTABLE SLEEPING

Next to your tent, your sleeping bag is probably the most important part of your camping equipment. Spend as much money on it as you can manage.

Most sleeping bags are filled with man-made fibres carrying such trade names as Terylene or Dacron. These fillings give adequate insulation for normal camping conditions but they tend to make the sleeping bag rather bulky for packing. For this reason, most lightweight campers use sleeping bags with a feather and down filling; they make quite a small pack for carrying but expand greatly when opened up (especially if they can be warmed in the sun for a few minutes), and give very good insulation.

Many bags have a zip fastener down one side and a short zip is certainly an advantage when getting in and out. There is little merit in a bag with a full-length zip for your type of camping. Remember that a zip is potentially a cold spot in your sleeping bag. The best bags have an insulated band behind the zip to cope with this problem. They usually have a draw string, too, so that when you are in the bag, you can tighten it around your neck to reduce heat loss through the top opening. A bag with a pocket sewn on at the top is useful. You can stuff the pocket with spare clothes and turn it into a pillow at night and the bag can be rolled up and tucked into the pocket for very compact carrying.

Sleeping bags are normally covered in either down-proof cambric, nylon, Terylene, or very fine cotton material. The man-made materials are easier to keep clean and marks can often be wiped off with a damp cloth.

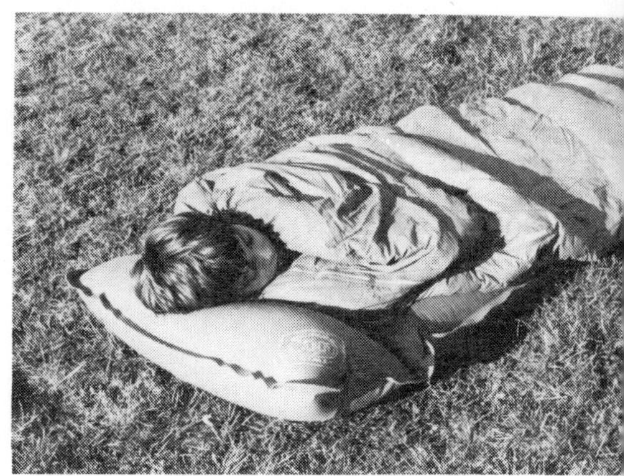

This is a quilted sleeping bag, Blacks Palomine, which has a filling of down and feathers and a down-proof cambric cover. This one has a 30-inch zip at the side. You can also get it without a zip. It weighs 4 lb. It is being used on a Kampamat, a comfortable foam mattress that weighs 2 lb 14 oz. The only disadvantage of this type of mat is that it is rather bulky when rolled up for packing.

The Blacks Icelandic sleeping bag has a filling of top quality fine duck down and feathers for extra warmth. It has special wall quilting to ensure that there is always a layer of down between the outer and inner fabrics. It has a draw-string round the neck to keep out draughts. It weighs 3 lb 2 oz and is available without a zip, with a 30-inch zip, or a full-length zip.

Simple quilting. Cold spots occur at stitch line where there is no thickness. Satisfactory for general purpose summer bags.

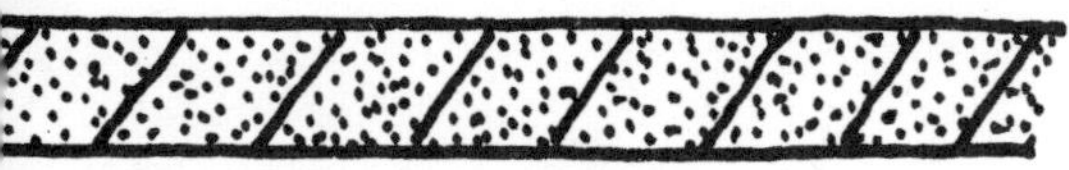

Walled quilting. An even thickness throughout gives no cold spots, while the walls give even distribution of down and allow for maximum expansion.

Overlapping tube construction giving best compartmentation and eliminating cold spots. Used for very low temperature and high altitude bags.

Types of quilting used with down-filled sleeping bags.

A convertible sleeping bag has a zip down one side and along the bottom. It can be completely unzipped and opened out for airing and for cleaning. It can also be used as a bed quilt at home and two zipped together form a double sleeping bag.

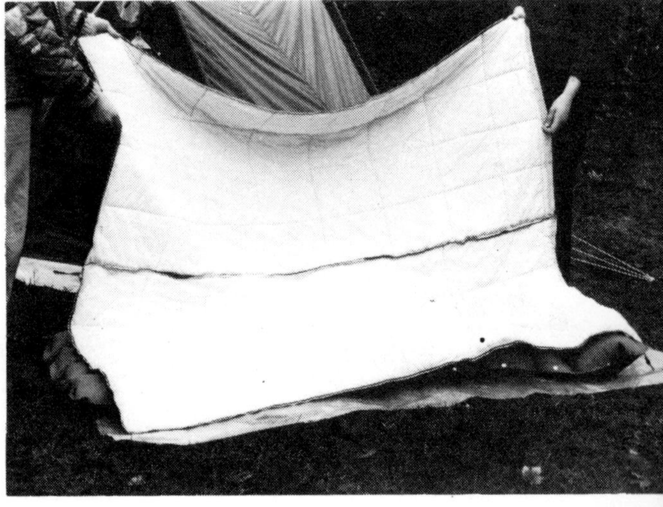

left: A zip fastener forms a cold spot in a sleeping bag unless there is an insulated strip inside the bag behind the zip. This bag does not have this special protection.

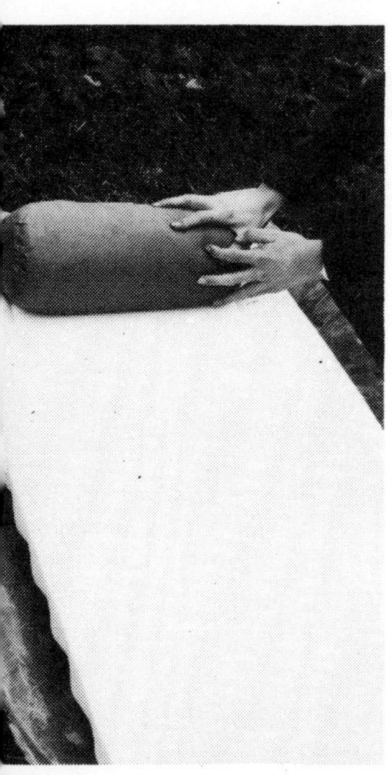

A down-filled sleeping bag rolls up very small for packing—

—but expands greatly on being opened up and becoming slightly warm. This gives excellent insulation.

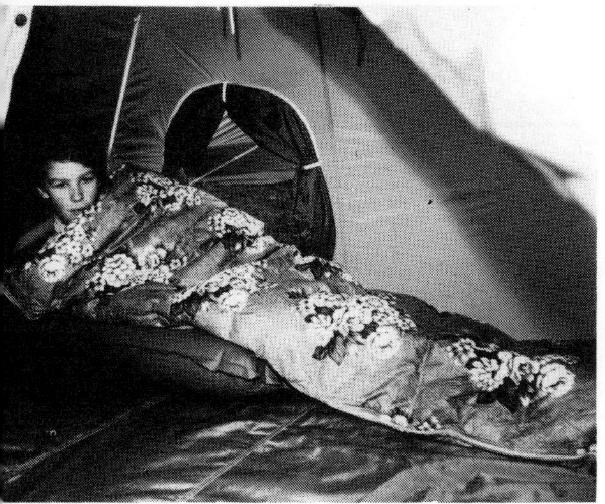

Some sleeping bags have attractively patterned covers. This one is being used in conjunction with a Good Companions air bed.

It is a good thing to use a sleeping bag liner of thin material inside your sleeping bag so that your body is not in contact with the bag itself. It is much easier to wash the liner than the bag. However, liners often seem to get twisted and tangled during the night. To avoid this, sew tapes on the bottom corners of the liner and the bottom corners inside the sleeping bag. You can then tie the liner to the sleeping bag at the bottom and the problem is solved. To keep your sleeping bag fresh and hygienic, take every opportunity of spreading it out in the sun to air.

If your sleeping bag does not have a pocket that will serve as a pillow, you can buy a small air pillow, but remember that it will not be very comfortable if you over-inflate it. Alternatively, carry an empty pillow case that can be filled with spare clothing.

You should have plenty of insulation under you to keep out the cold from the ground. Newspaper or brown paper is very useful but a thin woollen ground blanket is best, if you can find carrying space for it. If it covers the whole floor of your tent it will add considerably to your camping comfort. An alternative is a Space Blanket, made of a reflective material which is a virtual non-conductor of heat. You can pull it round you over your sleeping bag for extra warmth. It only weighs a few ounces and it packs very small. The crackling noise it makes as you move on it could disturb a light sleeper, and if you completely wrap yourself in it you may run into condensation problems.

Do not be ashamed to carry a hot-water bottle with you if you plan to camp in cold conditions. A hot drink just before you turn in is also helpful. So are extra clothes. Indeed, it is probably best to put on your sweater and even spare trousers tucked into your socks in order to be sure of staying warm in very cold conditions. But with a good sleeping bag in normal conditions, you should be snug and warm just with pyjamas on.

You will have to have your sleeping bag cleaned from time to time, and certainly at the end of the camping season, even if you use a sleeping bag liner. It is probably best and most convenient to have it dry-cleaned, but you must *never, never* get straight into a bag that has just been cleaned in this way. The cleanser produces poisonous fumes and people have died from them. So give it a good airing, turning it inside out, when it has just been dry-cleaned. Actually, most sleeping bags can be washed carefully, by squeezing them gently in a bath of warm water and a good soap powder. They can be spun dry but it is probably best to hang them up to drip dry, though the process is likely to be a slow one.

The pictures show a variety of sleeping arrangements that you can use in conjunction with your sleeping bag. Most air beds are fairly heavy and bulky but they do ensure very comfortable sleeping, provided they are not inflated too hard. The short air bed illustrated is long enough to support your back and hips, so it is a reasonable compromise if weight is a big consideration.

right: Another type of air bed, the convertible, can be used as a seat. It has three sections, the pillow, which forms the seat, and two sections which form the back-rest and back support. They are held in position by cords with hooks that go through holes in the back-rest and support sections. Note the foot inflator. Air beds should never be blown up by mouth. The moisture in the breath condenses inside and makes the sides of the air bed stick together.

below: A full-length reeded air bed in use and a Good Companions short air bed being pumped up with a small bellows hand pump. The short air bed is favoured by many lightweight campers because it weighs only $2\frac{1}{4}$ lb, about half as much as a full-length air bed.

below right: Don't inflate your air bed too hard or it will be uncomfortable to sleep on. You should just be able to sit on the ground through it for optimum comfort.

Foam mattresses are very comfortable, too, but their bulk presents a carrying problem.

Camp beds are too heavy and bulky to be seriously considered by lightweight campers.

The Bubble Pad, which only reached this country from the United States early in 1973, is a really light and very warm insulator, with just enough cushioning in it to keep the body off the ground. It is also very cheap and you can cut it or stick pieces together to give any shape and size you want. Since it is completely waterproof and non-absorbent, it is particularly useful for camping. Its bulk is about half that of a foam mattress and it can be carried outside your rucksack, wrapped in its own polythene carrier, and is usable as a seat when you stop for a meal.

The Bubble Pad, lightest for sleeping comfort and insulation, weighs only 12½ oz. It has over 1000 air bubbles and is surprisingly warm and comfortable. It is also very cheap.

COOKING AND LIGHTING

The very word camping conjures up visions of cooking over a cam fire, with the sweet smell of wood smoke hanging in the summer air. Unfortunately, pleasant as this type of cooking is, it is difficult to practise today. Very few camp sites permit fires, and many landowners are naturally reluctant to allow them because of the terrible damage that can be caused if a fire gets out of control. You may be lucky enough to find a landowner who will let you cook on an open fire and if you do, do not betray his trust by acting irresponsibly. Preferably, remove the turf from the area around your fire place, build a proper fire with logs or stones to support your pots, and make sure that the fire is completely extinguished before you leave it. When you strike camp, replace the turf so that your enjoyment leaves no scar on the countryside.

However, in the normal course of things one must expect to use a small stove for cooking. There are many such stoves available, using different fuels such as paraffin, petrol, methylated spirit, gas (butane) or solid fuel (metaldehyde). The selection of a suitable stove is largely a matter of personal preference, and will, to some extent, be influenced by the means of transport and nature of the camping expedition. To help in your choice, here are a few points to consider. Paraffin stoves develop a particularly fierce heat if required but are rather more difficult

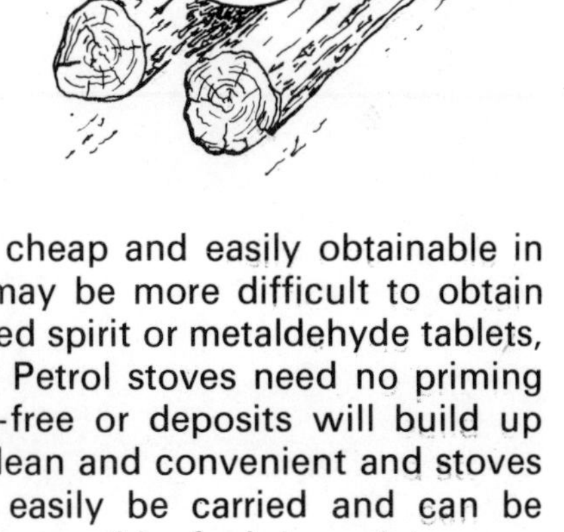

A Hunter's fire. Build it so that the wind blows along between the logs. Rocks or bricks can be used instead of logs.

to control for a small flame. The fuel is cheap and easily obtainable in Britain, but in some other countries it may be more difficult to obtain supplies. A second fuel, usually methylated spirit or metaldehyde tablets, is necessary for priming before lighting. Petrol stoves need no priming fuel, but the petrol used must be lead-free or deposits will build up around the burner and choke it. Gas is clean and convenient and stoves need no priming. Spare canisters can easily be carried and can be obtained easily all over Europe. However, this fuel is rather more expensive than the others. It is also less efficient in cold conditions.

Paraffin pressure stove. The fuel, pressurized by pumping, is forced up to the burner where it vaporizes for burning. The burner is preheated by burning methylated spirit in the trough below the burner. Flame size is regulated by varying the tank pressure with a valve. The vapour jet has to be cleared periodically with a pricker. The stove is dismantled and the tank capped to prevent fuel spillage for carrying. One-pint size is shown and a half-pint size is also available.

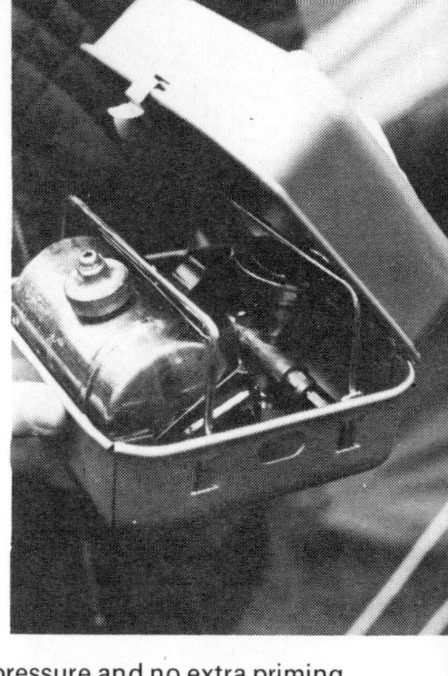

Another design of pressure stove. The large one (1 pint) runs on paraffin while the small one ($\frac{1}{3}$ pint) runs on unleaded petrol. The operation is the same as the other pressure stove but with petrol no pumping is necessary to create pressure and no extra priming fuel is required. The knob (obscured on the large stove) controls the flame height and also a built-in pricker. Note also the pot grips being used to hold the small saucepan, which is lined with a non-stick coating.

Methylated spirit stove. The fuel is in a tank in the lid and is vaporized at the burner. There is no wick. The knob controls the size of flame. Note also the bucket for holding water. It is narrower at the top than the bottom so that it is self-standing when full.

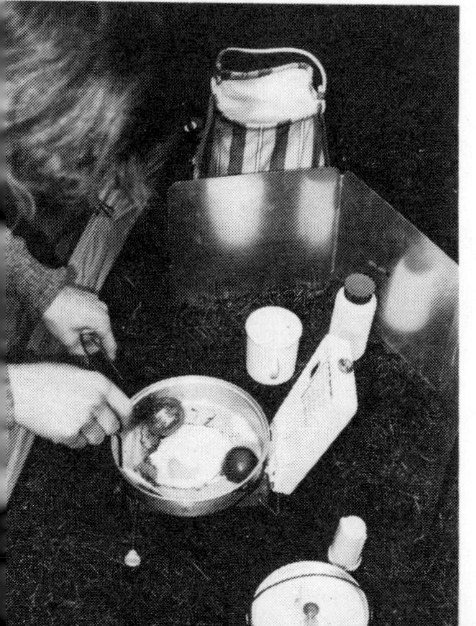

Solid fuel stove. Packs very small and compact into the saucepan and burns special tablets of fuel. Ideal for making a hot drink on a walk, but limited in scope for camp cooking.

Gas cartridge stove. One of many designs on the market that uses a sealed container of liquid butane gas. When fitted in the stove, the cartridge is punctured and must not be removed until empty. A regulator tap turns off the gas supply when not required and adjusts the flame height. A burner windshield and a base to stabilize the stove are useful additions. Note also the folding aluminium windshield around the stove, and the plastic egg box. The saucepan and dish beyond the windshield are part of the canteen and pack in the frying pan. The frying pan handle folds over to clip the canteen together.

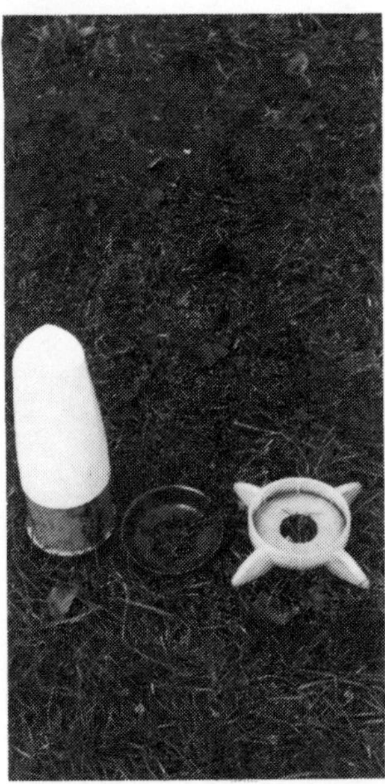

left: Another stove using a sealed cartridge of gas. When fitted, the control tap remains in place on the punctured cartridge, but the burner head may be changed for the lamp head.

right: Refillable gas bottle. These bottles are self-closing so that burners or lamps may be freely interchanged. When in transit the bottle is capped for safety using the cap lying between the lamp head and mug. Several sizes of bottle are obtainable; that shown is the smallest, holding 1 lb of gas. When empty, the bottle is exchanged for a full one. You pay only for the gas. Note the polythene water bottle which can be collapsed when empty for easier packing.

A wide range of meals can be prepared on these stoves, normally based on either boiling or frying. There are several canteens on the market, consisting of one or two saucepans with lids, a frying pan and plates that nest one inside the other to form a compact pack when not in use. When cooking in the open air, heat is soon lost so meals are best kept quick and simple, even though aids such as windshields can help limit the heat loss. However, meals must be sustaining and well-balanced and one of the arts of open-air cooking is to be able to produce a meal of two or three components on a single-burner stove, and have it all ready and hot at the same time. To give an example, consider a breakfast of, say, bacon, eggs and baked beans. The beans are heated first and then, still in the saucepan with the lid fitted, wrapped in a towel and put on one side. If the frying pan is not big enough for cooking both the eggs and bacon together, the bacon is fried next and placed in the saucepan with the beans to keep warm. Fry the eggs and serve the meal. The towel technique can be used for keeping other items warm, particularly boiled foods as the water will retain its heat.

Another trick is to stack a saucepan or deep metal plate on top of the cooking vessel. The cooked food is transferred to this covered upper container and keeps warm by the heat of further cooking in the bottom pan. Take care, though, that the stack is stable and will not tip over.

There is also an old campers' trick for pressure stoves. Because lighting paraffin stoves is rather tedious and uses up priming fuel, which is usually only carried in small quantities, the whole meal, hot drink and washing-up water are all prepared on a single lighting. To allow time to enjoy the after-meal drink, the pan of boiled washing-up water is left on the stove, the stove turned out and a tea towel draped over the water pan. This not only keeps the water hot, but dries the tea towel into the bargain.

One of the greatest boons to the modern camper is the availability of 'convenience foods'. Tinned foods, meats, vegetables, complete meals, puddings and fruit have been with us for many years and a big advantage about them is that they often only need heating up. However, they are sometimes too bulky and heavy to carry in quantity. Frozen foods offer an equally wide choice, but have a very limited life when kept outside a freezer. Never eat frozen foods after the period recommended on the wrapping. But if you are not too far from civilization and can buy these foods as required, they can provide a very quick and convenient meal, particularly those that are cooked in a plastic bag—much less washing up!

Dehydrated foods are probably the most useful to campers. Vegetables, soups and whole meals are available and all have the advantage of being light in weight and only requiring the addition of water for cooking. The most common vegetables such as peas, runner beans and mashed potatoes, as well as several complete meals, can be bought at most supermarkets, but specialist firms provide a much wider range of vegetables and also packs of selected expedition menus. Milk powder, instant coffee powder, tea bags, and even non-sugar sweetening tablets, can also simplify life at camp and reduce the weight of the rations that you travel with.

It is preferable to cook away from the tent, but bad weather will often force you back to the tent doorway. In these circumstances, a peg-out door, or a hood, awning or flysheet extension, makes life more comfortable—but never cook in a closed tent. The danger of a tent fire, a very rapid and deadly happening, is ever present and the possibility should not be taken lightly. While on the subject of safety, fuels should be kept in securely closed, labelled containers. With some fuels, such as petrol, it is a legal requirement that the container and cap are of metal. Empty gas cartridges should be treated with respect because although empty of liquid, they are still full of vapour. Change a cartridge well away from the tent and any flame; it is a wise precaution to completely fill the empty cartridge with water, so expelling all the gas. It can then be emptied out and safely placed in the rubbish bag.

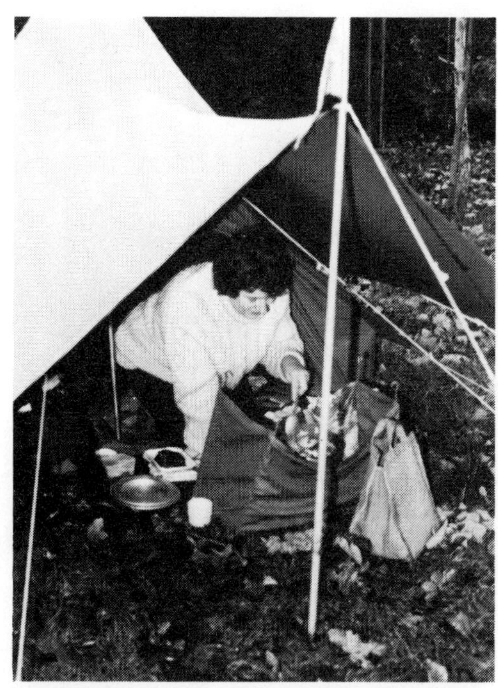

Meal in preparation in bad weather under a flysheet extension. Note the canvas windshield and wedge-shaped water bucket.

A hand torch is useful when moving about after dark but, because of its concentrated beam, it is not so convenient in the tent or for cooking by. Some form of lantern that will throw light in all directions is better. It can be battery-powered and the light produced is adequate for preparing for bed. However, at the time of year when the nights are longer, you may have to cook by artificial light, or wish to spend the evening reading. It is advisable to have a more powerful light for this. Paraffin pressure lamps are available but they are generally too heavy and bulky for use in small tents. A better choice is a gas lantern, which provides a very good light and also gives off heat. If you use it inside the tent, hang it up, if possible, as it could be dangerous if knocked over. Make sure that it is far enough from the tent roof not to damage it. Naked flames, such as candles, should *never* be used in a tent—the dangers are all too apparent.

Battery lamp. Hung inside a tent like this, it gives a good all round light.

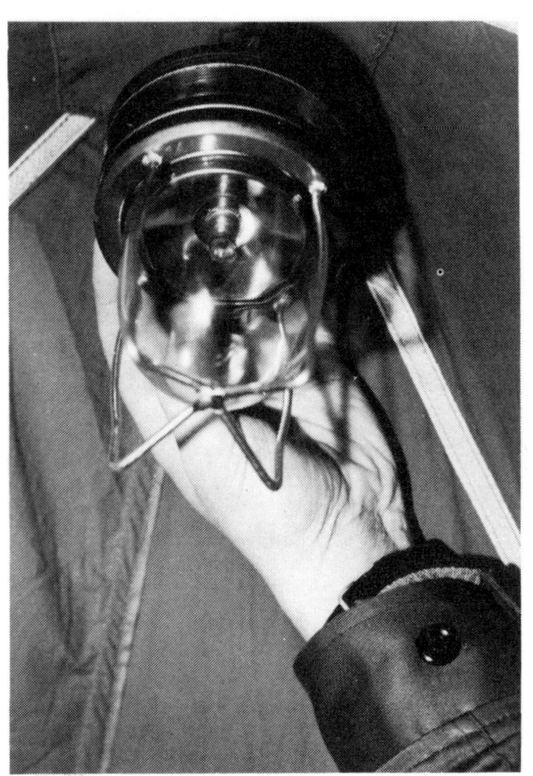

NEVER use a naked flame in or near a tent.

HYGIENE

Personal hygiene is very important in camp and a small nail brush should always be used when washing the hands.

The arrangements you will have to make about hygiene in camp depend on what sort of a site it is. Good camp sites provide first class sanitation; wash-rooms with hot and cold water, possibly showers, plenty of drinking water points and bins for rubbish disposal. Many of them also provide washing-up sinks and even laundry rooms.

But if you camp on farm land or away from all amenities, then you will have to make your own provisions.

You should carry a trowel or small camp spade and establish your sanitary arrangements when you pitch camp. At the minimum, you can dig a hole in a copse or some sheltered spot where your latrine will not be visible and where it will not create a nuisance to others. It is best to carry a toilet screen or a light toilet tent, especially if there are several of you camping together. Dig a hole about two feet long by one foot wide and around two feet deep. The pictures show you how to do it in such a way that, when you leave, the hole is filled in and the turf is replaced. Place two crossed twigs over it to indicate to other campers what it has been used for.

Dig a hole near to your camp and use it as a grease pit, where you can pour washing-up water, fat or any other liquids; they should never simply be thrown on the ground because this might foul it for use by other campers. Latrine holes and grease pits can be kept sanitary and fly-free by sprinkling them with a little disinfectant powder from time to time.

It is most important to be tidy in camp and not to throw litter or rubbish about. Keep it in a polythene bag and dispose of it properly whenever the opportunity arises. Empty tins can be made less bulky by opening both ends and then stamping them flat. They should never be buried because they are liable to be grubbed up by foxes or other animals and then they are a hazard to the feet of sheep, cattle or horses. Before you leave your camp site take a good look round and pick up every scrap of litter. This sets a good example to other campers and you will be welcomed when you come again.

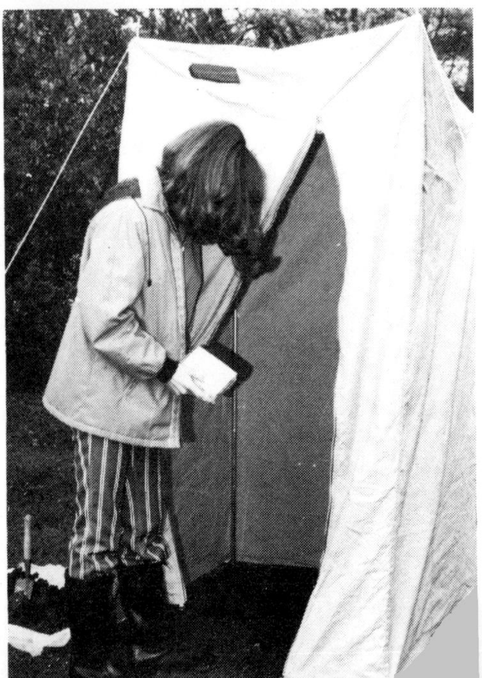

above left: Taking out the turf for a latrine hole or grease pit. Cut round the turf to be extracted with a small camp spade, and then carefully thrust the spade under it and ease it out.

above: Lay the turf grass-side-down near the hole. Dig out more earth to the required depth and place it on a polythene sheet, not on the ground. The bottom of the turf should be watered from time to time in warm weather to keep the grass alive.

left: A latrine hole should be dug about 18–24 inches deep and the toilet tent is then erected over it. The earth on its polythene sheet by the toilet tent is trowelled into the hole after each use. Note the flat pack toilet paper is in a polythene bag to keep it dry.

The grease pit is lined with twigs and grass so that grease accumulates on them and can be extracted and burned when necessary.

Rubbish should be kept in a polythene bag until it can be properly disposed of. The picture shows how the polythene bag should be slid between the strands of a guyline to keep it tidy and also to keep out nosy animals.

Good drinking water is available almost everywhere in Britain but you may occasionally camp in an area where you have to use stream or river water. A fast-flowing mountain stream is usually pure and drinkable but you can be doubly sure by carrying a little box of water-purifying tablets, obtainable from chemists for a few pence.

Always carry a first-aid kit with you. The one illustrated contains two bandages of different widths, several finger dressings, sticking plaster, pieces of absorbent gauze and boric lint, a packet of safety pins and some first-aid cream to be used on the dressings. Complete with a little booklet on first aid, it is a very handy little kit.

Adherence to these camping practices will ensure that your camping is hygienic and healthy as well as enjoyable.

Bandaging a cut finger. Note the small compact first-aid kit. It only weighs 6 oz in its waterproof wallet.

CLOTHING

For most camping almost any clothing will do. The important thing is to be comfortable, warm or cool enough, and dry. You should always have a selection of clothes to cope with different weather conditions. When the weather is hot, you may only want to wear a summer shirt and shorts, but have a pair of long trousers and a warm jumper with you for the cool evenings. A scarf is also good for that extra bit of warmth when it gets chilly. Girls will find trousers, jeans or shorts preferable to a skirt in camp, but they may like to take a skirt with them to change into if they are going out.

It is important always to have a complete change of dry clothes in case you are unlucky enough to get wet. Spare underclothes and socks take up very little space, but if you find that spare trousers, shirt and jumper are rather bulky, a track suit, which can also double as a pair of pyjamas, will provide a warm standby.

Jackets are not very suitable for camping and an anorak is a better garment. They have been designed especially for outdoor use such as camping, and are usually windproof, showerproof and fitted with a hood. Pockets often have zips or buttons so that money and other valuables can be kept safely. All in all, an anorak is a very useful article of camp clothing, but you may find that the padded ones are too warm in summer.

A plastic mackintosh is a wise extra for additional protection in heavy rain.

In dry weather any type of footwear can be used, but you must have some form of waterproof footwear; rubber boots or stout waterproof leather walking shoes or boots. It is amazing how quickly and completely ordinary shoes will be soaked through by walking in wet grass. Carry a pair of plimsolls or slippers to wear in the tent. Wearing your outdoor shoes or boots in the tent will make everything dirty and may damage your groundsheet. At night the boots can be stored in a polythene bag inside the tent.

A selection of anoraks. Note the zip-closed map pocket on the chest.

Wearing soft plimsolls while relaxing in the tent. Boots are left outside.

If you have to go outside the tent during a warm summer shower, try wearing just a swimming costume with bare feet or plastic sandals. When you get back to the tent you can soon towel yourself dry and get into some dry clothes—this is much easier than trying to dry wet clothing.

Later on in the book you will find essential clothing for extreme conditions described. As you gain experience you may find some of the more specialized clothing, such as cagoules and over-trousers, useful for ordinary camping.

Back-packing

The back-packer is probably the most versatile of all campers. He can get almost anywhere to camp, certainly to places beyond the reach of mechanical transport. Because his equipment is light and compact, he can travel by all forms of public transport, covering long distances quickly and easily. He can camp miles from civilization, or at popular holiday resorts. The possibilities open to him are immense.

A RUCKSACK TO SUIT

If you are going to carry all your camping equipment you will need some form of rucksack fitted with a frame. Frameless rucksacks can be ideal for rambling and carrying lighter loads, but when more is to be carried, a rucksack stiffened with a frame, which correctly distributes the load on your back, makes it much more comfortable.

Traditionally, a rucksack was cone-shaped with an A-shaped frame of metal or cane, but nowadays the 'high load' rucksack is preferred. There are two main types; the fitted frame and the pack frame. The former is a high load adaptation of the traditional rucksack, and is usually narrower at the base than at the top. In this way most of the load is carried as high as possible. The frame is not intended to be detached from the sack.

Pack frames originated from a type used by trappers. This frame was fitted with a harness so that separate packs, rolls and bundles could be lashed to it. However, with modern pack frames it is normal to use a specially fitted detachable sack for camping purposes. These are either the same size all the way up or narrower at the bottom, and as the frame can be extended above the shoulder straps, a head-high pack can be achieved. A waist strap attached to the bottom of the frame and fastening in front of the wearer can give a more comfortable carry.

Which type to buy is entirely a matter of personal choice; the right one is the one you feel most comfortable in but it is vital that you get one the right size. If it is too long it will chafe the buttocks and rock badly as you walk; if too short it will give you backache. A wide range of sizes is available, from about 16 to 22 inches, and some makes of pack frame provide an adjustment that can vary the effective frame size. When buying your rucksack, ask the shopkeeper to add some weight

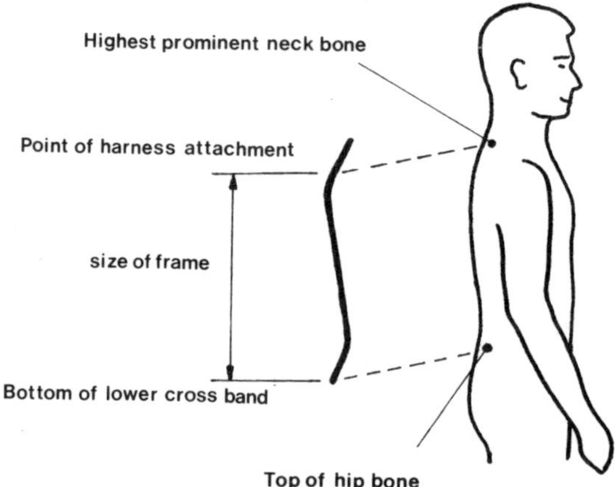

Getting the right size of rucksack. The distance measured on the back and the size of frame should be the same. When carried the frame will be 2–3 inches lower than the reference points on the back, so the crossband sits on the hips.

to it by putting in a couple of tents or something similar so you can make a better judgement. After all, this is how you will be using it.

The rucksack, of course, is part of the load you will have to carry so it is sensible to keep it as light as possible. The lightest ones are made with coated heavy-duty nylon bags and lightweight alloy frames but, as so often happens with camping equipment, it costs money to save weight, and you may find this too expensive, at least to start with. A canvas duck sack is just as serviceable but cheaper to buy. Check that the shoulder straps are well padded; if not, special shoulder pads can be fitted.

Different sizes of frame for different people. Note the frame extension below the pack frame on the left where a stuff sack can be strapped. The centre pack has a zipped entry to a lower compartment.

A fitted frame rucksack (centre) and two pack frames. The crossbar to which the shoulder harness is fitted on the frame on the left has an alternative position, 2 inches higher than illustrated, for taller people. Two frames (left and centre) have a shelf at the bottom so they are free-standing.

What is the best way to pack a rucksack? There is no pat answer to that; even old hands will disagree on detail, and this is quite natural when you realize that different people carry different equipment.

However, in working out your own packing scheme there are two golden rules. First, and most important, pack so that the weight distribution is correct and the loaded rucksack is comfortable. Secondly, pack so that items are in a convenient order for use.

The correct weight distribution is achieved by keeping the weight as high and as close to the back as possible. In this way the most upright posture can be achieved—apart from being the most comfortable, this has been shown by experiment to use up the least energy.

left: The right way. A well-packed high load allowing an upright walking position.

right: The wrong way. The combined centre of gravity of the man and his load is so far back that it is necessary to lean right forward to maintain balance. This is very uncomfortable and tiring.

Sometimes convenience in packing order agrees with the requirements of weight distribution. For example, the tent is one of the heavier pieces of equipment to carry, but as it is the first item required on arriving at your site and the last to be packed when leaving, it is best to pack it at the top of the rucksack. It can either be inside the pack or carried as a separate roll on top.

A sleeping bag is less straightforward to pack. For its bulk it is light, and so it should be at the bottom of the rucksack, with heavier items packed above it. However, this is probably the least convenient place for it. To lay out your bed you will have to completely empty your rucksack; clothes, cooking equipment and food supplies will all have

A helping hand to hitch on a load. Note the roll strapped on is in the best position, high and close behind the neck.

to come out, regardless of whether you want to use them or not. There are several ways around this problem. Some rucksacks are partitioned so that they are divided into upper and lower compartments. The lower compartment, ideal in size for a sleeping bag, is fitted with an outer zip so that it can be emptied without upsetting the packing of the upper compartment. Alternatively, the sleeping bag can be packed in a 'stuff sac'. This is a bag, usually of waterproofed nylon rather like a very small kit bag, that will just take a sleeping bag. This can then be attached to the outside of the load, either above or below the pack. With many designs of pack frames, the lowest part of the frame is not covered by the rucksack and the stuff sac can be strapped to this. When putting a down sleeping bag into a stuff sac, do not fold it first but simply stuff it in gently, starting with the foot of the bag. This is a very convenient packing method even if you intend to carry it inside the rucksack.

Polythene bags are invaluable when back-packing; wet or damp items can be isolated from dry bedding and clothing; fuel can be separated from food, preventing possible contamination; and damage of equipment from spilt fat or detergent can be avoided. Remember to pack your waterproof clothing in a side pocket or somewhere convenient in case of rain.

Some part of your journey will almost certainly be by public transport. There is usually no trouble when travelling by train, but with bus transport, attitudes vary from company to company. Some bus companies have no objection to rucksacks, others leave it to the discretion of the conductor, and some companies will not permit rucksacks at all. You may be charged a luggage fare. The usual objection is to the frame, particularly where there are prominent tube ends. This seems illogical when a folded push chair will be accepted, but one way around this is to detach the sack from the frame, stow the sack in the luggage compartment and then sit with the frame on your lap.

A CHOICE OF FOOTWEAR

When you carry a rucksack, the unaccustomed weight on your feet can result in jarring as your heel hits the ground and is also fatiguing. Stout footwear eases this, and in a way complements the load on your back, helping you to swing along in a nice steady rhythm. Ankles are particularly vulnerable. The best answer is a good pair of boots that not only give a broad base for stability but provide ankle support as well.

Boots need not be expensive, and good leather boots of traditional design can be obtained in most camping shops or 'surplus stores'. Nailed soles have now been almost completely replaced by composition rubber soles with a deep tread pattern, which have an excellent grip for walking, except on ice and compacted snow. The soles may be moulded directly on to the uppers or screwed and glued. Check with your supplier whether they can be resoled as it is important not to let soles and heels get too worn. The leather uppers should be regularly treated to keep them supple and waterproof by applying dubbin or other proprietary boot wax. If your boots do get wet, dry them gently and then reproof. Placing them over heat or in front of a fire can crack the leather. If the insides are wet, either from a soaking or from perspiration, stuff them with crumpled newspaper, or place a proprietary pack of dessicant in each boot.

Apart from the traditional design of boot, specially designed walking boots are also available, but these generally cost quite a bit more. They usually have a sewn-in bellows tongue which makes the boot waterproof up to the ankle, and a system of lacing using D-rings and hooks,

The back-packer's basics; boots and ruck-sack. Note the tread pattern on the composition rubber soles for grip and the internal padding around the top of the boot.

The bellows tongue of the boot opens out to make putting on easy with thick socks, but is sewn-in to make the boot completely waterproof. Note also the D-ring and hook lacing.

which is easy even with cold fingers. Other features can include a one-piece construction that does away with as many seams as possible to prevent chafing, an off-centre back seam for the same reason, internally padded uppers and tongue for comfort, and a soft padded top that gives a snug fit around the ankle without putting pressure on the Achilles tendon in the heel.

When you have bought your boots, do not go straight out on a long hike with a pack on your back. Your new boots will be stiff and your feet unused to them, so your feet will blister and be most painful.

Instead, go out for short walks, gradually extending them until your boots are sufficiently broken in and your feet hardened. Then you can tackle a camp with confidence.

Always wear a heavy pair of woollen socks with boots. Wear these over light everyday socks which can be changed and washed frequently. Wool is preferable to nylon or other synthetics as it absorbs perspiration more effectively. The use of foot powder is also recommended as it not only keeps the feet drier, but is treated with a fungicide to help prevent athlete's foot.

Since, as a back-packer, you rely on your feet to get around, it pays to look after them.

WEIGHT WATCHING

How much can the back-packer carry? This is a very difficult question to answer because so much depends on the strength, the fitness and the size of the individual. As a rough guide, a man is comfortable with about 30–35 pounds, women with 25–30 pounds and youngsters with proportionally less. While a person hardened to back-packing can carry more, and for short distances may even be able to double these loads, don't make the mistake of overdoing it. Many people, especially teenagers, will swing on a heavy pack and, because of bravado or a mistaken assessment of their own capabilities judged by a moment's wearing, set off full of confidence. The story is very different a few miles down the road. So keep the load light; after all, you are doing it for pleasure, not as a punishment.

Watching the weight does not mean that you have to leave essentials, or even some comforts, behind. There is no need to go to the lengths of cutting the handle off your toothbrush to save $\frac{1}{4}$ oz. Remember three guiding principles:–

Do not carry unnecessary items.
Choose the lightest alternative.
Share the load if possible.

When you return from a camp, separate everything into three heaps; things that you used, things you might have used if conditions had been different, and things that, in the light of the experience you have just gained from camping, you are unlikely ever to use. Next time, leave behind the third heap. Do this each time you camp, and your accumulated experience will weed out all the unnecessary items.

Choosing the lightest alternative when buying equipment speaks for

Vango Force 10 Mark 2 Featherweight. Nylon is used for the tent, flysheet and groundsheet. The side guyline also holds out the inner tent to give more room inside by means of a fastening between the tent and flysheet. The tent is supported by A-poles at the front, an upright pole at the rear and a ridge pole. When closed, the flysheet encloses a triangular storage area in front of the tent. Weight 6 lb 2 oz; length 6 ft 6 in; width, front 4 ft 3 in, rear 3 ft; height, front 3 ft 6 in, rear 2 ft.

Blacks New Solite in nylon. Weight 3 lb 15 oz; inner tent length 6 ft 6 in; width, front 4 ft, rear 1 ft 6 in; height, front 3 ft 6 in, rear 2 ft. No ridge pole is fitted.

Trio Troll. This tent has no flysheet and to combat condensation on the inside of the coated nylon, ventilators are provided in the side walls under the eaves and at the peak. Weight 3 lb 12 oz; length (front to back) 4 ft; width 6 ft 8 in; height 4 ft.

Japanese Caratent nylon tent with flysheet. The roof is supported with flexible glass-fibre rods that bend into hoops. Pegs are needed simply to hold it to the ground. It is fitted with a sleeve entrance on one side and a flap door on the other, with circular ventilators under the roof overhang. Weight 6 lb; length 6 ft; width 4 ft 2 in; height 3 ft 3 in.

Example of complete pedestrian camper's load ready for packing. It consists of rucksack, tent, sleeping bag, plimsolls, short airbed, electric lamp, petrol stove, cooking canteen, eating utensils, condiments, food (in polythene bags and containers), first-aid kit, sewing repair kit, spare trousers, sweater, underclothes, handkerchiefs, socks, shirt, waterproofs, towel and soap, tea towel, toothbrush, water bucket, map in map case, and compass. Total weight about 23 lbs.

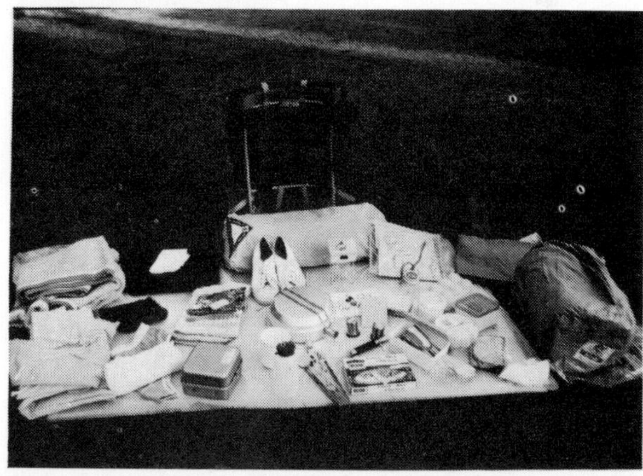

itself. When selecting a tent, a great deal of weight can be saved by choosing one made of nylon or other synthetic materials rather than cotton. This can more than halve the weight of your tent pack. Nylon flysheets are usually proofed with a urethane coating which is impervious to water or water vapour. For this reason the inner tent should be of a 'breathable' fabric, such as nylon with a silicone proofing and good ventilation to prevent condensation. Coated nylon groundsheets also save weight over the commoner reinforced plastic or coated fabric groundsheets. Unfortunately, tents in these materials are often considerably more expensive than their cotton counterparts. Lightweight alloy poles can also save weight, and for ease of packing they should nest if possible, one section inside another.

If two or three people camp together, they will only need one tent and one set of cooking equipment. Thus, by sharing, the load that each has to carry is less than if one were to camp solo. This is a good solution to the problem posed if the only tent available is rather heavy.

Cycle camping

If you decide to combine cycling with your camping, you will achieve a remarkable degree of independence and mobility. The cyclist will get a much better view of the countryside than the back-packer on the same road.

One obvious advantage of cycle camping is that the bicycle becomes the carrier of your camping equipment. This means you can carry a somewhat heavier and bulkier load than you would on your back—but don't overdo it. Remember that, if you cycle camp with companions, it is possible to share the load of camping equipment and keep the weight within reasonable limits whilst carrying enough for camping comfort. For example, a full-length air bed will always be manageable whereas a pedestrian camper might have to settle for a hip-length one. The seat air bed illustrated on page 27 is particularly suitable for cycle camping. A Terylene filled sleeping bag can be used instead of a down-filled one, with some saving in cost. If the tent is to be shared between two or three people, a quite large one with fairly high walls, which add tremendously to usable space, can be carried by splitting the total load three ways, into tent, flysheet and poles. Only one cooking stove, with fuel, and one set of cooking equipment needs to be carried.

The combination of cycle and camping equipment to suit you is very much a personal choice. However, it can be said that small-wheel bicycles are less suitable than large-wheel ones for load carrying. You will find that a bicycle with 27-inch steel rims (heavy gauge spokes), and 1⅜-inch tyres is very suitable for cycle camping, though many prefer 1¼-inch high-pressure tyres despite the harder ride that they give. A lightweight frame of 531 tubing is very suitable and the choice of saddle and handlebars will depend a good deal on your size and weight. Remember that the bicycle will carry an extra load of perhaps 30 pounds, so that brakes must always be maintained in very good condition. Give them a test flick before you start a downhill run, because the momentum from the extra weight is quite considerable.

Gears are particularly important on the bicycle you use for camping. You will need a really low bottom gear to enable you to keep riding up a fairly steep incline, fully loaded. Something in the lower 30s is appropriate and it is probably best achieved by a combination of 5-speed derailleur gear and double chain wheel, giving a choice of ten gears and enabling you to cope with most conditions. Make sure that you overhaul your cycle regularly and replace worn tyres, bearings and chain as soon as necessary. It is very awkward if you break down a long way from home with a full load of camping equipment.

The loading of your cycle is particularly important for good balance and proper control. Pannier and other carrier bags are obtainable in strong lightweight proofed material and these help to keep down the weight of your total load.

They must be strapped to strong purpose-built pannier carriers over the front and rear wheels. Use one front pannier for your cooking

A well-loaded cycle for a cycl camper. Note the large rear pannie bags and the tent in a polythene ba laid across them, supported by th pannier carrier. The front pannie bags are very useful for food, cook ing utensils, cycle repair kit, etc. Th handlebar bag can be used fo shopping. Note the stove clippe on the crossbar, the lamp forwar of the front pannier carrier and th multi-gears to cope with a heavil loaded bicycle in all conditions.

This is a badly loaded cycle. All the weight is concentrated at the rear and this upsets the steering. In any event, a rucksack is quite unsuitable for use with a bicycle.

canteen, cooking and eating utensils, food containers, condiments, water bucket, etc. and the other for your cooking stove and fuel, dish cloth, tea cloth, pot scourer, soap, washing-up liquid and disinfectant powder. If you use a saddlebag as well as rear panniers, the saddlebag can carry spare clothing, food, cycle cape and leggings, and repair kit. One rear pannier will take the sleeping bag, air bed and camping accessories whilst the other will take the tent, flysheet and groundsheet. The poles, in a separate bag, may have to be placed across the carrier and anchored under the saddlebag. Rubber 'spiders' or elongated guylines are useful for this purpose and can be used for anchoring a plastic sheet as protection over your cycle at night. Alternatively, you can dispense with a saddlebag, carry your tent and flysheet, in its carrying bag and a polythene bag, across the rear pannier carrier, and use the second rear

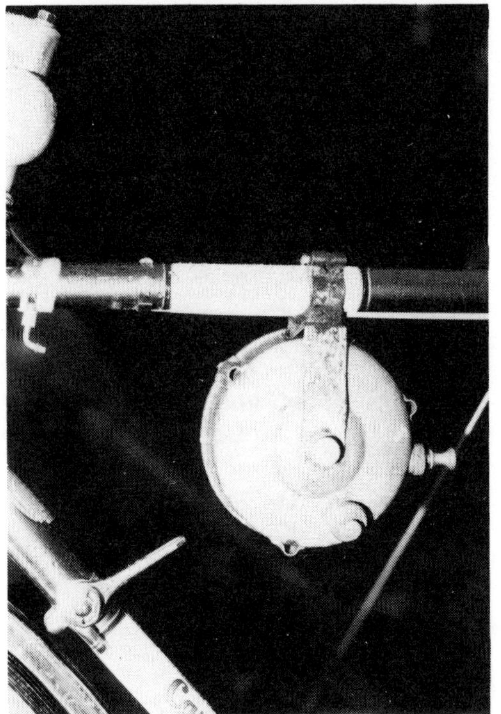

Making a bicycle stand up in camp. All you need is a piece of guyline and two pegs. Peg down one end, wrap the guyline round the crossbar several times and then peg down the other end tightly with the bicycle balanced between the two pegs.

Primus stove fuel tank clamped to crossbar by special bracket. This is a good space saving device and there is no fear of the paraffin contaminating food or clothing.

pannier for spare clothes, possibly on top of canned foods which should be packed at the bottom to keep the centre of gravity as low as possible.

However you pack, be sure to keep stove and fuel away from foods, and damp articles away from dry ones. Have your cape easily accessible at all times and remember that your tent has to be pitched as quickly as possible in bad weather so it must be easily get-at-able.

A small bag slung on the handlebars is very useful for carrying a packed lunch, the snacks you want to eat en route, small items of shopping and maybe your valuables, camera and maps. It is a wise precaution to take this bag with you whenever you leave your cycle unattended.

Maps are invaluable. The Bartholomew half-inch is ideal for general use and Bartholomew or Ordnance Survey one-inch for areas you intend to explore in depth. You can also get tremendous fun from planning with the aid of these maps. You don't have to follow your plan precisely but it gives you good ideas of what you may find.

It is a good idea (and relatively inexpensive) to take your loaded cycle by train to the starting point of the main area you want to explore. Remember that you may have to remove all baggage and equipment and carry it, so take suitable cord or straps for the purpose. They always come in handy anyway.

After a little experience, you may well want to camp abroad and this can be great fun. Again, use boat and train to cover the long distances.

Plan on a day's ride of sixty to a hundred miles when cycle camping but don't worry if you only do twenty, as long as you enjoy it. The great attraction is the freedom you have, so make the most of it.

Canoe camping

Canoeing and camping are a particularly enjoyable combination. By definition, canoeists get away from the crowded places, on canals, rivers, lakes and estuaries. By adding camping equipment you are able to stop overnight in remote areas, on riverside camp sites, lock islands, by towing paths, on lake shores and the little uninhabited islands in many estuaries. In fact, in some of the finest spots for really self-contained camping.

If you want to canoe camp, you should choose a canoe that is fairly broad in the beam; a single should have a beam of up to 30 inches and be between 13 and 15 feet in length; a double should have a 32 to 36-inch beam and a length of 17 or 18 feet.

Canoe camping in a two-seater canoe with an experienced canoe camper is a very good way to learn.

It is vital that you pay very great attention to safety from the outset.

Make sure that the canoe has permanent buoyancy at both ends. This can take the form of air bags or rolls, lumps of polystyrene or other buoyant waterproof material pushed into the nose and stern of the canoe, under the deck. There should be stem and stern loops to which are attached life lines, running the length of the canoe, and painters for mooring, for towing the canoe and for lining it down shallow and rough water. You should wear a life-jacket of approved style at all times when canoeing and, if possible, fit your canoe with a spray deck which will minimize the amount of water that comes inboard, even in quite rough or choppy waters.

You should certainly learn to swim and consider in advance the best thing to do if you should have the misfortune to capsize. Remember that your canoe, if it is upside down, is full of air and will therefore float

Canoeing at Llyn Gwynant, Wales.

indefinitely. So, if you are wearing your life-jacket and are able to grab one of the life-lines, you can drift with the canoe, kicking towards the shore or river bank, until you ground and are able to scramble out and right the canoe.

You may never capsize but you must plan for this possibility. You must also store your camping equipment with the same possibility in mind.

This means that everything has to be packed in waterproof bags; tent, clothing, cooking equipment, sleeping bags and air bed, etc. The stout polythene bags used for rubbish storage are excellent for this

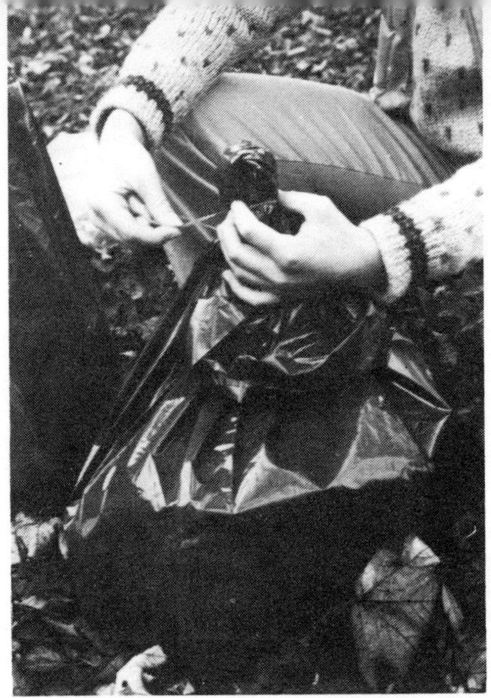

above left: Everything belonging to a canoe camper should be packed in waterproof bags. Stout polythene bags, such as those used for rubbish collection, do very well. Close them with a rubber band, taking care to leave some air in, so that, if they fall overboard, they will float. Screw the top of the bag tight, turn it over on itself and band it tightly.

above right: Packing a canoe. The best storing points are at the front and rear of the canoe under the decks. The waterproof bags with some air left in act as buoyancy bags too. Note the life-jacket being worn.

purpose but various sizes of heavy gauge polythene bags will prove useful. Do not fill the bags completely. Leave quite a bit of air in, seal them with a rubber band, then turn the tops over on themselves and seal them again. They will then be waterproof and will have their own built-in buoyancy. How you actually store your kit will depend on the size of your canoe, but in general you will push your equipment in its waterproof bags into the nose and tail of the canoe, under the deck. You will quickly learn the shapes and sizes of packs that will fit in and suit your packing accordingly. If you have difficulty in extracting

Safe launching. Two people edge the canoe off the bank and drop it into the water. Note the paddles laid across the gunwale. They can be used to stop the canoe floating away if the painter is not tied up to something on the bank.

Safe embarkation. The boy holds the canoe firm whilst the girl gets in. She sits on the bank, puts her feet in the centre of the cockpit, grasps the gunwale with her left hand, steadies herself with her right hand on the bank and moves gently in.

packages from the extreme ends of the canoe because these are long and narrow, tie a cord round the necks of the bags, leaving the ends accessible, so that you can tug them out when you reach your camp site.

Because your canoe will support a great weight of equipment you may be tempted to carry a lot but remember it all has to be stowed when you break camp and disembarked when you pitch again. Remember, too, that the heavier the weight, the harder it will be to paddle, and if you have to portage, or take the canoe out of the water and carry it round a rough or dangerous stretch, it will be hard work. Incidentally, if you think this is likely to happen, it is a good idea to carry a small canoe trolley with dismountable wheels. One end of the canoe is strapped on the trolley and it is then relatively easy to carry the other and steer the canoe wherever it has to go.

It is quite a good idea to attach small waterproof bags under the gunwale on each side of the canoe, just beyond where your knees normally fit. You can keep your personal belongings and valuables, your picnic food for the day, camera and other things you need in them.

It is also a very good idea to carry one or two collapsible plastic water containers full of drinking water. These containers are very tough and quite cheap and they have a loop handle so that you can tie them into the canoe. With your own drinking water supply and a trowel for sanitary purposes, you can make camping more exciting by choosing really remote spots or uninhabited little islands.

The girl is using her paddle with one blade pressed over the gunwale and the other pressed on the bank to hold the canoe steady whilst her partner embarks.

Safe disembarkation. Whilst the rear paddler holds the canoe steady by the bank, the front paddler raises himself with a hand on each gunwale, then, keeping his weight as central as possible, moves gently sideways, bottom first. When his bottom is on the bank, he can then rotate and bring his legs ashore.

In a broad, long two-seater canoe it is possible to stow a kit bag or frameless rucksack in the centre of the canoe, anchored behind the front seat. It is also possible to give yourself the comfort of pillows in camp, using them as cushions to sit on (in their waterproof bags, of course) when you are afloat.

Canadian canoes with raised ends and no deck provide a lot of carrying space but little protection from weather, water splashing in, etc. They tend to accumulate water in the bottom so it is as well to ensure that your kit is raised an inch or two off the bottom and wrapped in a waterproof sheet as well as waterproof bags. It should be anchored to the canoe, too, in case of capsizes.

When you have learned how to embark and disembark safely, how to store your camping equipment and how to paddle effectively, you will want to know about the waterways you are able to use. Edward Stanford Ltd., 12 Longacre, London W.2, publish a map showing British navigable waterways with their locks, and another showing possible waters for canoeists. The British Waterways Board also publishes information on the more popular waterways.

Remember that you have to have a Thames Conservancy licence if you plan to canoe on the Thames above Teddington, and that most

Paddling away. Note the drip sheets over the lap of each paddler and over the gunwale. Even with drip rings on the paddles, some water is bound to come inboard. Many canoes can be fitted with a spray deck which leaves a small cockpit in which the paddlers sit. A waterproof joint between paddler and spray deck is formed by a wide belt of deck canvas, elasticated top and bottom. The top grips the waist of the paddler and the bottom is edged over the rigid rim of the cockpit.

canals require a licence, issued by the British Waterways Board Pleasure Craft Licensing Office, Willow Grange, Church Road, Watford, Herts.

If you want to learn about the best ways of canoe camping in Britain, consider joining the Camping Club and its special section, the Canoe Camping Club. Its members are very experienced canoe campers.

Mountain camping

The mountains have a beauty and a fascination all their own, particularly to those who love walking or that 'away from it all' feeling. However, they also have their special dangers, ready to trap the unprepared and inexperienced. Camping in mountains not only requires skill in camping techniques but also in mountain craft. Camping skills can be learned and practised in the safety of the lowlands, and we shall consider how these can be adapted to high-level camping. Mountain arts, though, are beyond the scope of this book, and it is debatable whether they can be learned from any book except for basic principles. They should be learned practically in the company of experienced mountaineers. One of the best ways to visit the mountains for the first time is in a party with a suitably qualified leader. In Britain, it is strongly recommended that this leader should hold a Mountain Leader's Certificate issued by the Central Council of Physical Recreation. Alternatively, join a mountaineering club, or holiday at a mountain school or training centre. The mountains are no place for the foolhardy, but with experience and by taking the required safety precautions you can enjoy most rewarding and satisfying holidays in safety.

As a first step, consider some of the dangers and how they are overcome. A main hazard is weather. Temperature drops with altitude at between three to five degrees fahrenheit for each 1,000 feet. Wind cools the body further, and if clothes or skin are wet, this also lowers the body temperature. Inadequate protection against this cooling can result in exposure, which is difficult to diagnose and, if untreated, is fatal. Suitable protective clothing should be worn. Boots, similar to those described earlier, must be worn but if a composition rubber sole

Protective clothing. A knee-length waterproof nylon cagoule provides excellent protection in rain. Note also the *stop tout* (waterproof gaiters) worn over the boots.

is used, make sure that it is a reputable mountaineering sole and not an industrial sole, which may grip on oily concrete but not on wet rock. Flannel, woollen or cord trousers are satisfactory but jeans should not be worn as they offer next to no protection when wet. You may prefer to wear climbing breeches and long socks. If you wear shorts you should carry trousers with you in case the weather worsens. String vests, long shirts and sweaters will provide adequate thermal insulation to the body, but a windproof anorak should always be carried or worn. The anorak may be inadequate in rain, and a coated nylon cagoule and over-trousers, which are light and fold up small in your pack, are invaluable. If wearing breeches, gaiters or *stop tout* are a useful addition, particularly in snow. Top clothes, such as cagoules, should be in a bright orange colour as this will stand out most in conditions of poor visibility.

Warm headgear and mits should also be carried. In winter, further protection will be required. Never be misled by good weather when you set out; in the mountains weather can change very rapidly, even in apparently settled conditions. Always be prepared for bad weather or cold, but don't wear more than necessary as this can lead to exhaustion.

Another danger is poor visibility. Fog, mist or cloud can blot out your route so always carry a one-inch or two-and-a-half-inch to a

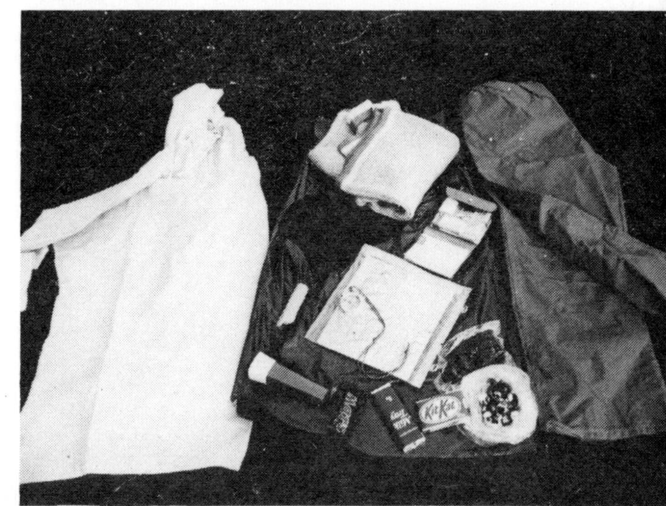

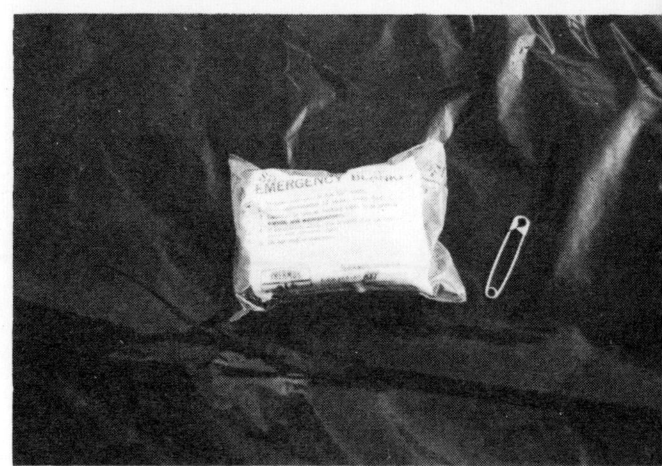

The minimum that must be carried on a walk in the mountains: spare clothing, first-aid kit, map, compass, whistle, torch and emergency rations. The reflective blanket is not essential but is a wise precaution. In an emergency it will keep a person warm by reflecting back and thus keeping in the body heat. It is also waterproof.

mile scale map and a good compass, and really make sure you know how to use them both properly. If on a walk and forced to spend a night on the mountain away from your base, be prepared by carrying emergency equipment; rations, extra clothes and shelter.

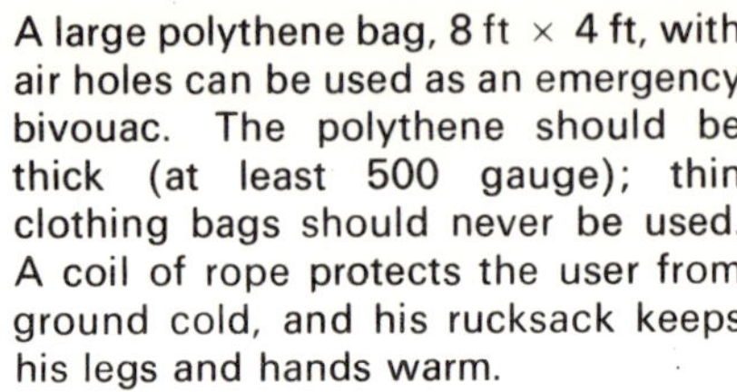

A large polythene bag, 8 ft × 4 ft, with air holes can be used as an emergency bivouac. The polythene should be thick (at least 500 gauge); thin clothing bags should never be used. A coil of rope protects the user from ground cold, and his rucksack keeps his legs and hands warm.

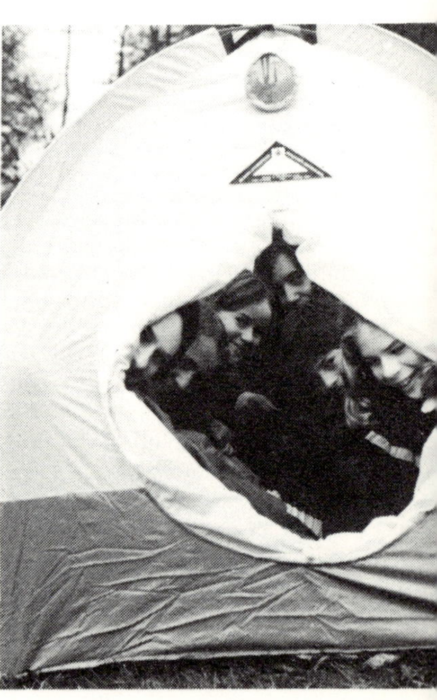

Blacks Survival Tent. This can provide emergency shelter for a whole party; the picture shows six people inside. It is of proofed nylon with a sewn-in tray groundsheet and is supported on flexible fibreglass hoops. It has a sleeve entrance and four sleeve ventilators. Weight 5 lb; length 5 ft; width 5 ft; height 3 ft 3 in.

These safety precautions are necessarily a very short summary and are certainly not complete. If you are interested in further reading, the

C.C.P.R., 26 Park Crescent, London W.1 publish a very good booklet, *Safety on Mountains*, which goes into more detail and lists mountain training centres.

The actual art of camping in the mountains is little different to good camping anywhere, but it does require some modification, particularly regarding the type of tent you use. Here are a few pointers on how to adapt.

When camping in the mountains, comfort takes second place to survival, and tents should be specially designed for mountain camping, particularly at high altitude. The fabric used must be strong and the design such that it can withstand high winds. The groundsheet should be sewn-in, preferably in the form of a three- or four-inch deep tray. Pegs are often kept to a minimum as they may be difficult to insert in rocky ground, and a valance should be fitted so that it can be weighted down with rocks.

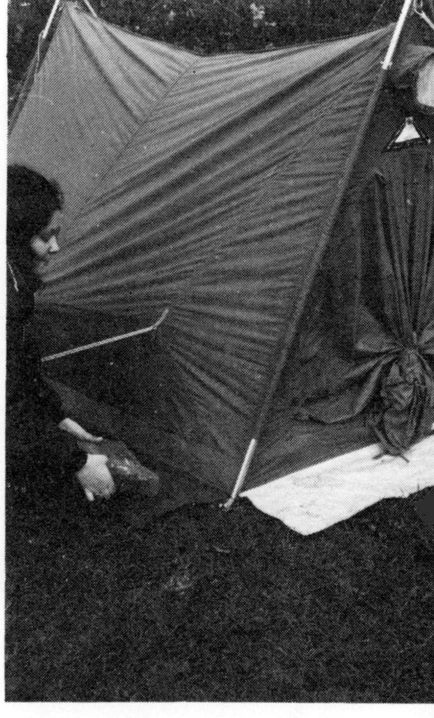

Blacks Mountain Tent. A-poles at each end fitted in pockets make this a sturdy tent and the side guys, which can be fixed to a single peg on each side, give a wall effect for more comfort. Note the tunnel door, the tubular ventilator that can be tied closed and a wide snow valance. Weight 15 lb; length 7 ft; width 4 ft. A flysheet is also available.

Blacks O.B. Venture. A mountain te[nt] designed for adventure training school[s]. It is similar to the 'mountain tent' but has flap doors and the groundsheet is n[ot] sewn-in. Weight (with groundsheet) 16 lb; length 7 ft; width 4 ft 8 in; height 4 5 in.

Ultimate tent. A streamlined tent with sewn-in groundsheet. The tent and flysheet do not separate and are pitched together in one operation for simplicity. There is a three-sided bell at the front with a door on each side. The fabric is silvered on the inside to prevent heat loss.

Pitch your tent in a sheltered spot with the doorway to leeward. Make sure of good drainage as water can collect remarkably quickly in heavy rain. No matter how cold or wet you may get, always cook a hot sustaining meal once you have changed. Dry your wet clothes as much as possible and wear them next day while walking to keep your spare clothing dry as long as possible. In the cool of the evening you may find a down-filled padded jacket, known as a duvet, a useful addition, and be sure to use a good down-filled sleeping bag.

lacks Tunnel Tent. Supported by sec-onal fibre-glass hoops, this tent also has tunnel entrance, sleeve ventilators, a ewn-in groundsheet and a snow val-nce. Weight 8¾ lb; length 7 ft; width 4 ft in; height 3 ft 3 in.

.M.F. Tyrolia Gale Force. The twin A-ole and ridge pole make a very stable ame for this tent. The flysheet is of coated ylon and the inner tent of nylon or cotton. ne 6-inch walls are held with rubber guys tting onto the flysheet pegs. Note the ay groundsheet and snow valance eighted with rocks. Weight, all nylon) lb, with alternative cotton tent 12 lb; ngth 6 ft; width 4 ft 3 in. The flysheet as an 18-inch deep triangular bell at each end for storage, reached through zip doors in the tent.

Once you have made the effort and gained experience, the rewards are limitless. The mountain areas offer an incredibly wide range of opportunities for the outdoor enthusiast and lover of the wild; nature

Good companions with their Good Companions tent camping by Llyn Ogwen, in the Nant Ffrancon Pass, North Wales.

studies, geology, fell walking, rock climbing, winter and very high altitude activities. As your experience of the mountains grows, so will your respect and your love of them.

Wild camping above Nant Ffrancon Pass.

Gadgets and comfort

Camping is like many pastimes; by learning basic skills you can be a good camper from the beginning, but it is something that you never stop learning. The more you camp, the more you learn little 'tricks of the trade' or devise gadgets or improve your equipment with your own modifications so that your camping becomes even more enjoyable. All this can be regarded as making life under canvas more comfortable.

A very useful modification, for instance, is to provide your tent with a 'front porch'. Extra protection in the form of an extended flysheet keeps otherwise exposed tent doors dry in rain, creates a very effective cooking shelter, and gives extra shade in hot weather. With a ridge tent, this modification is carried out by sewing an extra panel of tent fabric to the front edge of the flysheet and supporting it on a third pole. Suitable guylines will then hold it so that it follows the shape of the flysheet. If an eyelet is fitted to go over the front tent pole, the extension can be completely separate from the flysheet and need only be rigged up when required. Extra doors or a bell end can also be fitted to the flysheet or extension. With single-pole tents, the principle is similar, but it may be a little more tricky to design.

If you plan to camp in hot weather, a mosquito netting door, a standard item on some tents, can be fitted so that you can have full ventilation at night without being bothered by insects. Fit it on the inside of the normal doors, and arrange it so that either set of doors may be used with the other set neatly rolled back and tied.

There is always the difficulty of looking after small items in a tent, particularly valuables. Stowage pockets, made from tent fabric, can be sewn to the inside walls. However, only do this on the wall of a tent

An extended flysheet for a ridge tent. This is an easy modification and can be made to most ridge tents.

A home-made modification to a Good Companions flysheet, giving excellent weather protection at the front and providing an under-cover cooking and storage space. The normal twin guylines have been removed and a ridge tape substituted. The front edge is the same height as the tent doors and is supported by a line to the pole which is a foot or so in front of the extension to give easier access.

Mosquito netting doors are useful in hot weather. Note the ordinary door rolled and tied up.

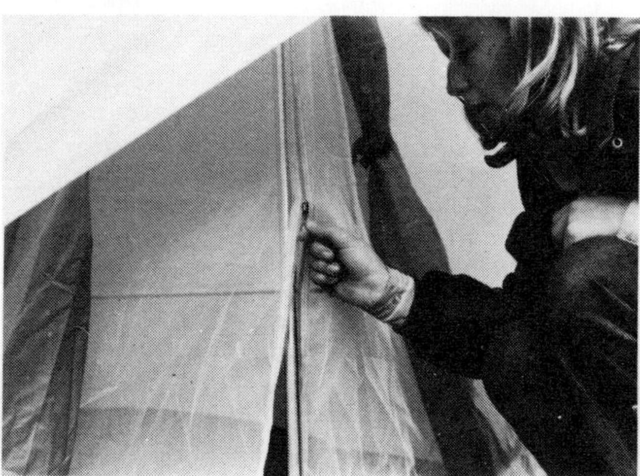

where there is an eave on the outside to carry the water away from the tent and, of course, do not sew it to the roof or through the rising part of a tray groundsheet. Store only small, light articles in these pockets; heavy or bulky items will pull the tent out of shape.

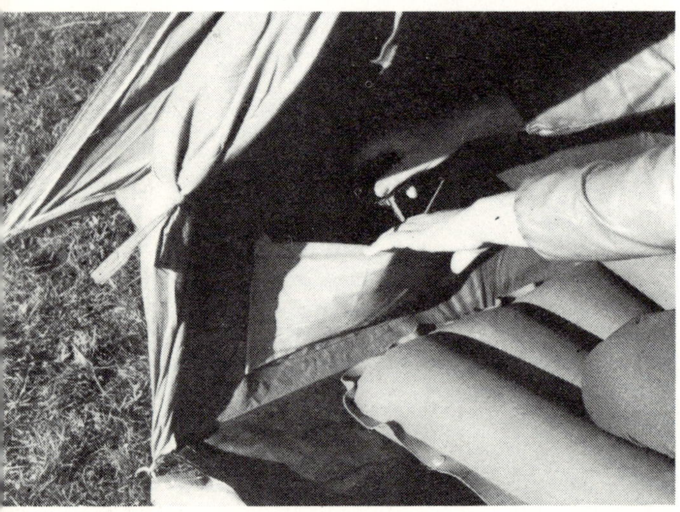

A stowage pocket sewn to the inside of the tent wall—ideal for storing small items and valuables while in the tent.

If you want to hang clothes up to dry or to keep neat, never hang them from a ridge pole as it is not designed to take this type of strain. Make up a line of the right length with an aluminium ring at each end that will fit over the upright poles before positioning the ridge pole. Alternatively, use spring clip hooks that attach to upright poles. Another clothes line to use outside for drying tea towels and so on can be made from two lengths of elastic lightly twisted together. If articles are trapped between the two strands, no clothes pegs are required.

A complaint often made about camping in small tents is that sitting on the ground for long periods becomes most uncomfortable. This is such a basic problem that it was solved many years ago by the invention of the stirrup backrest. This was used seventy years ago by T. H. Holding, who was a pioneer of mobile camping and founded the first-ever club for camping, and it is possibly an older idea than this. Yet surprisingly it is seldom seen today. To make the backrest take about a yard of webbing two or three inches wide and fix an eyelet or a ring into each end. To each of these attach a length of cord, fitted with a runner so it can be adjusted like a guyline. To use it, sit on the ground, place the webbing round the small of your back, place a cord 'stirrup' over each foot and adjust them until they are tight when your legs are nearly straight. Then lean back. It is surprising how comfortable this simple device is. You will soon find the best adjustment to suit yourself.

Clip-on hooks fitted to an upright pole can be put up or removed in seconds. This is a good way to hang up clothes or equipment. The mirror is unbreakable polished metal.

A stirrup back rest—a surprisingly comfortable gadget.

A useful camp bowl. Draw a line around the bottom of a cheap polythene bucket using a mug or similar to keep the line an even distance (4 or 5 inches) from the base. Cut along the line with a sharp knife. The bowl is ideal for washing up, upside down it can be used as a small table for eating, as a rain cover for a water bucket or cold stove, and it can be packed by fitting over the end of a sleeping bag.

Another gadget you can easily make yourself is a bowl cut from the bottom of a cheap plastic bucket. It has a range of uses and does not collapse as folding canvas bowls tend to.

While on the subject of camper's tricks, there are several relating to keeping food cool. Apart from the insulated bags and freezer packs now available, some items, such as drinking water, can be kept cool by standing them in the shade under the flysheet, but not in the tent where the air gets hot. Alternatively, food boxes or drink bottles can be kept in a hole in the ground, or in a cool stream, or wrapped in a damp towel. One of the most effective ways of keeping dairy produce fresh is to stand it in a bowl with water in it and to drape a wet cloth over the food containers and into the water. The food is cooled by evaporation of water from the cloth, which is kept wet by the water soaking up it from the bowl.

Insulated food bag keeps food cool and fresh. It also keeps food away from possible contamination and prevents foods such as butter from spreading onto spare clothes or camping equipment.

You can add to the effectiveness of your insulated food bag by using a frozen coolant. Taken from a deep freezer, a coolant like the one in the picture will keep food cold in the insulated bag for 24 hours. The coolant can be refrozen in the camp shop's deep freezer.

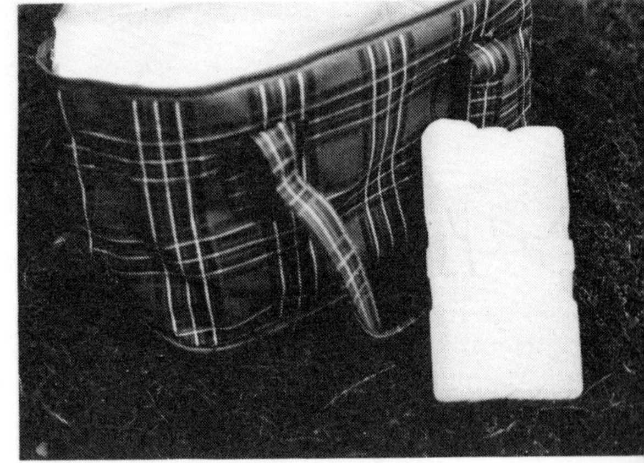

Simpler cooling. A milk bottle standing in a pan of water and covered with a tea towel that dips into the water. As the water evaporates, it cools the milk bottle.

A wise camper soon learns to carry with him a collection of items to effect temporary repairs and the like; sewing materials, spare runners, rubber guys and pegs, a gadget knife, and so on. Nylon cord is particularly useful as it can be used for such things as storm guys, washing lines and boot laces. A small tear in canvas can be temporarily patched to prevent it from running further with an adhesive plaster from the first-aid kit. A broken pole can, with luck, be bound with splints as an emergency measure. If a small leak in the canvas develops, it can be stopped from dripping by drawing a wet track with a finger from the leak straight down to the eaves. This, of course, only stops the drip and not the leak.

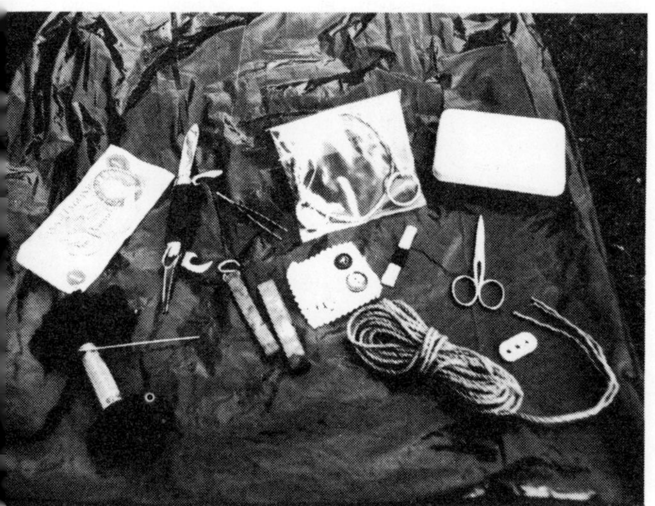

A selection of useful items enabling you to cope with almost any contingency: camper's knife, tweezers, tiny flexible saw, first-aid kit, pound note, spare rubber guys, buttons, safety pins, needle and cotton, scissors, darning wool and needle, strong guyline, spare runner.

It is much better, though, to guard against the possibility of having an emergency repair by maintaining your equipment. After a camp, check for any wear and correct it before it gets worse. Air tents and sleeping bags well before storing. Replace broken and lost pegs and straighten bent ones. Reproof your tent whenever necessary. Thoroughly clean your stove. Be as thorough as you can. There is no substitute for this type of maintenance, and looked after properly, your equipment will give you many years of faithful service.

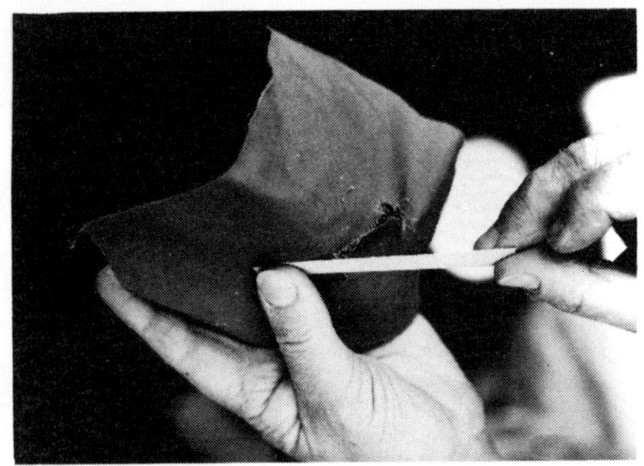

above: Repairing a small tear in canvas with a plaster from the first-aid kit.

right: Splinting a broken pole in an emergency.

In this chapter you will find a mixture of tips and ideas. Try to think up some of your own, though this will become easier as you get more camping experience. How about a removable tray groundsheet held in place with touches of Velcro all round? This should give advantages of both sewn-in and loose groundsheets and will allow brailing up of the walls to air the inside of the tent. We do not know anyone who has tried this yet, but it might work!

When you're experienced

PROFICIENCY TESTS

The Camping Club of Great Britain and Ireland has a special section called Camping Club Youth, specifically for young campers between the ages of twelve and eighteen. Most of the pictures in this book were taken with the assistance of CCY members, nearly all of them very experienced campers.

The aim of the CCY is to give training in good camping practices so that the young campers trained by experienced instructors quickly become proficient and self-reliant.

They are expected to camp at Camping Club sites or with sections of the Club where practical assistance and advice is given to them.

After a period of instruction and practice they are encouraged to take a camping test. They have to arrive on a camp site carrying their own kit in a rucksack or on a bicycle. They then demonstrate that they can pitch their tent correctly, that they can assemble and light their cooking stove and prepare a meal on it. They show that they camp tidily and hygienically and they answer questions to demonstrate that they know the Code for Campers devised by the Camping Club.

Having passed their test, they are awarded their special CCY Test Pennon and their membership card is suitably endorsed. They are now regarded as competent to camp on their own, on private sites as well as Club sites. They are entitled to attend the Camping Club Youth Annual Rally and the International Youth Rally and, in fact, they are usually very responsible young citizens because of their training and the self-sufficiency they have developed.

Part of the Camping Club Youth test. Campers must be tidy, but 'you musn't bury your rubbish' says the instructor.

Instead, you should keep it tidily in a polythene bag and dispose of it at the camp site disposal point.

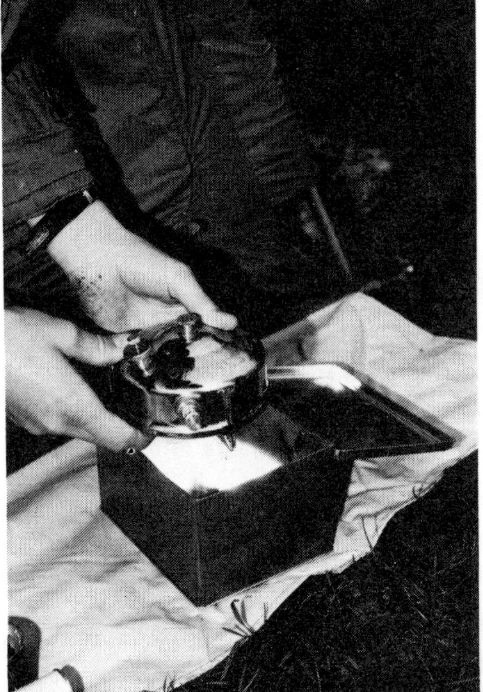

One of the CCY tests is to assemble a pressure stove, fuel it and light it correctly.

The test pennon awarded to young campers who have passed the Camping Club's CCY test.

When you have applied the advice, tips and information in this book, you too should be a similarly competent camper and responsible member of the community.

WINTER CAMPING

To many people, especially those who do not camp, this sounds horrifying, but when you have enjoyed summer camping and become skilled at it you will realize that it can be very enjoyable and you need not suffer.

Obviously one needs to keep warm, so you will need extra clothing and either a very good sleeping bag or an extra blanket. The smaller your tent, the easier it is to keep warm as there is less air in it, but do ensure adequate ventilation. A down-to-earth flysheet also adds warmth, and if it has a closing bell end at the front, so much the better. The ground will strike cold, so try to sleep on an air bed, foam mattress or bubble pad that will lift you off the ground. It is a good idea to sit on your bed when cooking. A reflective blanket is useful if spread over the groundsheet as this helps to keep ground cold at bay.

A gas lantern is worth having as with long dark evenings you will need a good light, and it will also provide heat. For safety's sake, do not leave it unattended, do not leave it alight while you sleep, and make sure that it cannot be knocked over.

Expert tuition in the art of camping being given at Capel Curig by instructors from the Central Council for Physical Recreation Centre at Plas y Brenin.

Where have all the campers gone? Under canvas, every one. Winter camp in Edale, Derbyshire with Kinder Scout in the background. Note the doorways pegged out to shelter the entrance and minimize heat loss in the tent.

Cook good, hot sustaining meals and drinks, but keep them simple so that you do not have to remain inactive for too long. Stews, hot pots, soups, cocoa and porridge are ideal in winter.

Before you pitch, clear the ground of snow if possible. If snow falls once you are pitched, leave it in place on the tent unless the weight of it is too much and threatens to collapse the tent or stretch the material. Snow is a very good insulator and a light layer will help to keep the tent warm. Mountain tents are usually better constructed to take a snow loading. Find a pitch with good shelter and drainage; high winds and heavy rain are likely in winter as well as snow. If the ground is already covered with snow, make sure that it is very well drained by probing with a stick, as local flooding can easily occur with a thaw. In winter, drainage can only be achieved on sloping ground. When the earth is frozen or water-logged, water will not soak away.

Finally, a warning; mountain camping in winter is strictly for the very experienced with qualified leadership. Conditions, even in British mountains, which are small compared with others in the world, are extreme. But there is a great deal of fun and adventure to be had from camping in less dramatic surroundings in winter, with the normally green fields and trees covered in a mantle of white.

INTERNATIONAL CAMPING

Camping is a very international pastime and it enables many young people to travel extensively at reasonable expense in all the countries of Europe, North America, North and South Africa, Australia, New Zealand, and even Japan where camping is rapidly growing in popularity.

If you belong to one of the Clubs affiliated to the FICC (Federation Internationale de Camping et de Caravaning), and you have shown your competence as a camper, you have the opportunity to camp at the International Youth Rally referred to in the caption to the picture. Many international camping friendships start through contacts at the International Youth Rally and through meetings on camp sites and they are some of the added pleasures that you may derive from your camping.

With air transport getting cheaper and easier, it is now possible to travel to countries you once only dreamed about, and because you are now well on the way to becoming a really competent lightweight

International Youth Rally. Young campers from several countries gather in a corner of the British area of the annual International Youth Rally organized at Easter each year by one of the member countries of the International Federation of Camping and Caravanning.

camper, you will be able to take full advantage of these opportunities and those presented by cheap student flights, rail and boat travel.

With good camping equipment and the know-how in this book, the world is your oyster. Happy Camping!

Code for good camping

Wherever possible, camp on private land rather than waste land, and always ask for permission. Conform to any directions or regulations of the site owner or local authority. In remote areas, where the landowner may be difficult to locate, check up on local regulations before setting out.

Do not light wood fires without permission, or break down hedges or trees for firewood. Avoid lighting fires or throwing lighted matches or burning cigarette ends near dry grass or bushes. Be particularly careful near forests and plantations.

See that your lighted stove does not set fire to surrounding grass. Never leave a lighted stove or lamp unattended in camp.

Leave no litter at all. If there is no proper rubbish disposal, take your rubbish home.

Do not commit a sanitary nuisance.

Always be courteous to your hosts and neighbours in the countryside.

In the country, leave all gates as you found them, open or shut. Take care not to damage crops, wild flowers or woodlands.

In camp, do not invade other people's privacy and camp well away from other tents.

Do not make any noise that could be a nuisance to anyone else. The rule is absolute silence between 11 p.m. and 7 a.m.

Always camp as well as you can and try to set a good example to others.

Equipment check list

You will not need all the items listed here and you may wish to add some of your own. Tick off each item as you pack it to make sure you leave nothing behind.

Tent
Groundsheet
Flysheet
Pole(s)
Separator(s)
Ground plate(s)
Pegs
Peg extractor
Guylines
Polythene sheet
Carrying bag(s)
Spare line and runners
Extra pegs

Sleeping bag
Sleeping bag liner
Air bed
Inflator
Foam mattress
Bubble pad
Air pillow
Pillow case

Soap
Flannel
Nail brush
Tooth brush
Tooth paste
Towel
Washing-up liquid
Dish cloth
Pot scourer
Tea towel
Polythene bags
Clothes pegs
Camp spade
Trowel
Toilet tent
Toilet paper

Night clothes
Spare clothes
Track suit
Swimming costume
Boots

Ground blanket
Space blanket

Cooking stove
Fuel for stove
Primer fuel
Pricker
Spanner
Windshield
Matches
Canteen of pots and pans
Pot grips
Cutlery
Tin/bottle opener
Plate
Cup
Food containers
Water container
Water sterilizing kit
Insulated bag
Freezer pack
Bowl
Lantern
Fuel or battery
Spare lamp mantle

Foot powder
Dubbin
Plimsolls
Anorak
Waterproof clothes

Rucksack, cycle bags or canoe bags
Map
Map case
Compass
Torch
Batteries
Whistle
First-aid kit
Repairs kit
Tent pole hook (clip on)
Mirror
Stirrup backrest

Food

Money